FROM HERE
TO
ATTORNEY

The Ultimate Guide to
Excelling in Law School
and Launching
Your Legal Career

J. Robert Arnett II
Arthur Coon
Michael DiGeronimo

Professional Publications, Inc.
Belmont, CA 94002

From Here to Attorney

Printed in the United States of America

ISBN: 0-912045-53-1

Library of Congress Catalog Card Number: 92-62828

Professional Publications, Inc.
1250 Fifth Avenue, Belmont, CA 94002
(415) 593-9119

Current printing of this edition (last number): 6 5 4 3 2 1

Table of Contents

PREFACE. v

ACKNOWLEDGMENTS vii

PART ONE: Choosing a Law School and Getting In 1

    Chapter 1: Do You Actually Want to Be a Lawyer? 3
    Chapter 2: Getting into Law School:
              What You Need to Know and Do 9
    Chapter 3: Choosing a Law School that is Right for You:
              The Basic Considerations 19
    Chapter 4: Considerations Involved in Part-Time Law School Study 27

PART TWO: A Basic Law School Primer 31

    Chapter 5: The First Year of Law School:
              Debunking the Myth 33
    Chapter 6: Study Aids:
              The Dos and Don'ts of Outside Reading 47
    Chapter 7: Studying for and Taking the Law School Exams 63
    Chapter 8: Choosing Second- and Third-Year Courses 79

PART THREE: Law School's Extracurricular Activities 83

    Chapter 9: Maintaining a Life Outside of Law School 85
    Chapter 10: Law Review, Law Journals, and Moot Court 89

PART FOUR: Law-Related Employment 101

    Chapter 11: Job-Hunting Tips for the Law Student 103
    Chapter 12: How to Find Legal Employment 119
    Chapter 13: Judicial Clerkships 133

Professional Publications, Inc. • Belmont, CA

PART FIVE: The Bar Exam 141

              Chapter 14: Studying for and Taking the Bar Exam 143

APPENDICES. 149

              Appendix A: Formal Brief 151
              Appendix B: Course Outline 153
              Appendix C: Course Mini-Outline 177
              Appendix D: Class Flowchart 187
              Appendix E: Sample Exams 191
              Appendix F: Résumé and Cover Letter 209

ABOUT THE AUTHORS 211

Professional Publications, Inc. ▪ Belmont, CA

Preface

"Experience is a hard teacher because she gives the test first, the lesson afterwards."

— Vernon Law, former pitcher, Pittsburgh Pirates

The best way to explain law school is by analogy to a game, the rules of which are not known or made available to the players until after the contest starts. The rules of the law school game are, unfortunately, learned only as play progresses. Consequently, law school, especially that crucial first year, is often frustrating and unpleasant for its players who achieve scores far below the level of their abilities. This, however, does not have to be the case. This book, written by three lawyers who have played the law school game and won, offers a complete set of insider's instructions for playing the game before it starts. These instructions are designed to help the reader excel academically and enjoy law school at the same time. We also provide other critical information that will help the reader do better academically and advance toward a satisfying legal career.

We believe that a fair amount of well-directed effort can make the law school years some of the best of your life. With this premise in mind, we have organized this book into five major sections. These sections comprehensively cover the steps required to take you from aspiring law school applicant to full-fledged lawyer.

The book's first section begins by offering advice on choosing and getting into a law school that is right for you. Contrary to what you may have heard, there is no "best" law school for every student. Selecting and getting admitted to the right law school for you are among the most

Professional Publications, Inc. • Belmont, CA

important things you can do to make your law school years successful and rewarding.

The book's second section provides an introduction to the hectic and sometimes bizarre world of the overwhelmed and underinformed first-year law student. The basic rules of the law school game are set forth in detail in this section: what to expect in the way of classes, workload, professors, fellow students, and tests; how to study for and take law school exams; how to prepare for daily classes; and how to decide which supplemental study materials you should buy and which you should avoid. This section also discusses second- and third-year courses.

The third section of the book focuses on law school's extracurricular activities. It emphasizes the importance of keeping a balanced perspective by maintaining a social life outside of law school, and it discusses some problems peculiar to the ever-growing group of part-time law students. This section also tells you everything you will need to know about those infamous institutions of moot court and law review so you can make informed choices about whether and to what extent you may wish to participate in those activities.

The fourth section of the book covers a variety of concerns law students have after they finish their first year. It offers advice on applying and interviewing for jobs in an increasingly tight legal market, obtaining summer clerkships and employment after law school, working part time during the course of your legal studies, and pursuing judicial externships and clerkships.

The fifth and final section concludes the book with some helpful caveats about preparing for and taking the much-dreaded bar exam, the first "trial" each law school graduate must win in order to become an attorney-at-law.

We are certain that the information contained in this book will assist you in many ways throughout your law school career. While certainly not intended as a substitute for hard work, the book levels the law school playing field by providing its readers with one all-important and previously unavailable advantage: knowledge of the rules of law school before play begins.

J. Robert Arnett II
Arthur F. Coon
Michael E. DiGeronimo

Professional Publications, Inc. • Belmont, CA

Acknowledgments

The authors wish to acknowledge the assistance and encouragement of the individuals and organizations without whose help the writing of this book would not have become a reality. We would like to thank our respective law firms of Miller, Starr & Regalia and Cades, Schutte, Fleming & Wright, with particular thanks to Eugene Miller, Esq., for their encouragement and support throughout the years. We gratefully acknowledge Shari Santos, Michael Lasseigne, Lorie Smersfelt, Cindy Hinckley, Sharon Moore, and Susan Kerr for their assistance in typing seemingly endless drafts of the manuscript. Thanks also to Laura Barrett Coon for her insightful comments and assistance in research and gathering of reference materials. We further thank Michael Hassen, Esq., and Professor Steven H. Shiffrin for their generosity in reviewing and suggesting improvements to the draft manuscript, along with the many other friends and colleagues who provided comments, insights, and suggestions as the work progressed. Finally, we appreciate the patience and perseverance of the editorial staff at Professional Publications, Inc., especially Jason Standifer and Jessica Whitney.

While acknowledging the helpful contributions of these individuals and organizations, we would also like to emphasize that the views and opinions set forth in the book are those of the authors only, who are solely responsible for its content.

J. Robert Arnett II
Arthur F. Coon
Michael E. DiGeronimo

PART 1

Choosing a Law School and Getting In

Chapter 1: Do You Actually Want to Be a Lawyer?

Chapter 2: Getting into Law School:
            What You Need to Know and Do

Chapter 3: Choosing a Law School that is Right for You:
            The Basic Considerations

Chapter 4: Considerations Involved in
            Part-Time Law School Study

Do You Actually Want to Be a Lawyer?

"The first thing we do, let's kill all the lawyers."
— Dick the Butcher in Shakespeare's
King Henry VI, Act IV, Scene ii

So you think you want to go to law school? Welcome to the club. Did you know that the United States has more lawyers, both in total numbers and per capita, than any other nation on this earth? California alone has in excess of 133,000 lawyers. In 1988, Census Bureau and American Bar Association data indicated that one of every 328 persons in California was a lawyer. New York had a lawyer to total population ratio of 1:234, and the Massachusetts ratio was 1:212. This country is teeming with attorneys, making the status of lawyerhood a little less rare, exotic, and highly regarded than many would-be Clarence Darrows might imagine.

There are a number of possible reasons for this country's lawyer boom. The United States is the world's largest and oldest existing democracy, based on the blueprint of an aged but ingenious legal document—the Constitution—drafted by a lawyer, James Madison. Our country is founded upon principles of free speech, equality under the law, the rule of "laws not men," and the right to representation in government. Each of these principles encourages an atmosphere of robust debate, cogitation, and argument. This atmosphere has created a legal system and tradition of unparalleled size, strength, and complexity. Consequently, a lot of lawyers are needed to tend to this magnificent system.

Given our rich common law legal heritage from England, and the judiciary's coequal constitutional status in our tripartite system of government, it was probably inevitable that lawyers would proliferate in the United States. Our free-market system, economic wealth, and growing population have further nourished a bumper crop of lawyers with legal issues and disputes of ever-increasing complexity. In their zeal to regulate, state and federal legislatures as well as local governmental entities have increased the demand for lawyers by enacting countless statutes and ordinances, all of which must be drafted, interpreted, enforced, and applied—usually by lawyers.

Some reasons people seek to enter the legal profession include perceived status, power, and money. There is no doubt that knowledge of the law confers power and status in this society, but, as the introductory quote from Shakespeare shows, this should not necessarily be confused with societal respect. Likewise, many practicing lawyers do make phenomenal (and seemingly unconscionable) amounts of money. Starting salaries in 1991 for first-year lawyers at New York's biggest and most prestigious law firms were approximately $85,000 per year. Partners in the country's most prestigious law firms routinely receive draws measured in hundreds of thousands of dollars per year. Still other lawyers earn contingency fees upward of a million dollars for services rendered in connection with a single case.

Of course, only a very small percentage of lawyers can ever hope to obtain such high-paying jobs or to strike it rich for their work on a single case. In reality, most lawyers work for a net hourly wage that is at best above average. Accordingly, if your aim in seeking a legal career is to become wealthy, there are probably much easier and better ways of accomplishing this goal.

Personal power, status, and money are only part of the equation, however. Many would-be lawyers are persons of lofty ideals who see the legal profession as an effective means of changing societal flaws and injustices and combating crime, pollution, and other problems. Such persons want to use the law to make a positive difference in our world. Some people see the law as a gateway to other professions, like politics or government service, where the same beneficial ends can be pursued. Our adversarial system of justice also attracts individuals who enjoy the competition, high stakes, and occasional drama offered by the cases lawyers handle. Still others appreciate the challenge and satisfaction of structuring the complex business arrangements that afford certainty and stability to our society's economic transactions. In short, there are probably as many motivations for becoming a lawyer as there are lawyers themselves.

Furthermore, the legal profession has many rewards. Closing a hard-won deal, settling or winning an important case, or devastating an untruthful witness on cross-examination can be very exciting and satisfying. The job of a practicing attorney, at its best, is also intellectually stimulating. Unlike assembly-line work, the work lawyers do usually varies from case to case. Many cases lawyers work on require them to learn about such complex and diverse fields as medicine, architecture, and engineering. In short, the variety, challenges, and intellectual stimulation offered by the practice of law can make for a very fulfilling career. Furthermore, few other jobs offer the opportunity to fight city hall (or even the state and federal government) and win!

Being a lawyer or just earning a law degree can also provide flexibility in terms of career choices and everyday life. The law has always provided a sure pathway to numerous jobs in the fields of business, government service, and education. Also, as a practicing lawyer, you will generally have control over when you arrive at work and when you leave. You will have considerable, and eventually complete, autonomy in handling your cases. All that your boss, associates, or partners will care about is whether you get the job done, not whether you are at your desk at any given moment.

Deciding whether you want to embark upon the arduous path of becoming a lawyer is not a decision to be taken lightly. Some lawyers find it amazing that anyone would want to become an attorney, since a lawyer's life is sometimes quite miserable. Most attorneys work very long hours, often on weekends. The pressure and stress lawyering generates can be tremendous—hectic calendars and travel schedules; difficult, unappreciative, and nonpaying clients; hostile, rude, and overaggressive opposing counsel; endless demands to bill more hours to increase firm profits; blown business deals (often blamed on lawyers); constant deadlines and a resulting "putting out fires" mentality; and endless conflicts with family life—such is the practicing lawyer's lot. In a recent opinion poll taken by *California Lawyer* magazine, a startling 70 percent of the lawyers surveyed said they would start new careers now if given the option! Seventy-two percent said they enjoyed practicing law less now than when they began, and 73 percent would not advise their children to become lawyers.

Moreover, do not expect that becoming a lawyer will win you any popularity contests with future acquaintances, or even your own clients. Public opinion of lawyers always seems to be at its nadir. It is difficult to pinpoint the reasons for the low esteem in which the public holds lawyers, but many persons unjustly identify all lawyers with a few unethical shysters or ambulance chasers. Insurance industry propaganda and tort reform campaigns have undoubtedly added to the public's negative perception of lawyers as a whole. Many individuals feel (with or without justification) that their attorneys have mishandled a matter for them, and these people always seem more vocal than the many satisfied clients. Even clients who have received excellent services and results from their lawyers may become dissatisfied when they get the bill, feeling that since they were right after all, why should they have to pay so much for "simple" vindication?

A certain amount of resentment at the legal profession is undoubtedly justified. Our legal system is so complex, and lawyers are now so expensive, that the average middle-class person is effectively denied access to the nation's courts for resolution of his legal disputes. Whatever the reason, though, for the public's low perception of lawyers, be prepared to tolerate those ever-present lawyer jokes.

> *What's the difference between a dead lawyer and a dead skunk on the road?*
> There are skid marks leading up to the skunk.

> *What do you call 500 lawyers at the bottom of the ocean?*
> A good start.

> *What's the difference between a lawyer and a vulture?*
> The lawyer gets frequent flyer mileage.

Hilarious, right?

The point of the foregoing remarks is neither to encourage nor dissuade you from pursuing a career in law, but instead to underscore that the decision to go to law school should be made with great care and for reasons that truly appeal to you. The decision should not be rushed. Consider working for a law firm part time as a legal assistant (or *paralegal*), receptionist, secretary, or clerk before applying to law school to get a taste for the type of work involved and the legal environment in general. Do not make the mistake of relying on "L.A. Law," "Equal

Justice," "Matlock," "Perry Mason," or some other Hollywood fantasy for your vision of the legal profession.

However, after you have carefully considered the implications and alternatives and are convinced that you want to go to law school, do not let the large number of existing lawyers change your mind. Though competition for the top legal jobs is indeed fierce and increasing (which is one of the reasons you should pay careful attention to the employment-related chapters of this book), there is still a demand for lawyers and people with legal training in our society. So if you are convinced you really do want to become a lawyer, by all means read further, and remember the sound advice once given to one of us: "Every profession, no matter how crowded, must make room for those who are good at it."

Professional Publications, Inc. • Belmont, CA

Getting into Law School: What You Need to Know and Do

"But, good gracious, you've got to educate him first. You can't expect a boy to be vicious till he's been to a good school."

— Saki (H.H. Munro)

Once you have made the commitment to study law, it is time to engage in some self-assessment and planning. The traditional path to law school and eventual lawyerhood requires a bachelor's degree (BA or BS). While it is still theoretically possible to gain entry to law school without a bachelor's degree, or even to qualify to sit for the bar exam without ever going to law school (at least in California), the requirements for doing either are extremely difficult to meet. The odds against successfully completing either endeavor following such nontraditional routes are also exceedingly great. Assuming, then, that you want to attend one of the 175 ABA-accredited law schools in this country, what do you do next?

General Overview

All law schools judge applicants on a number of factors, but two are most important: undergraduate grade point average (UGPA) and Law School Admissions Test (LSAT) score. For those of you who did not graduate from college magna cum laude or summa cum laude, take heart. While you may have missed your chance to go to law school at Harvard, Yale, or Stanford, there are still plenty of excellent law schools within your reach. If you carried substantially less than a B-average through college, your chances of entering the better schools are certainly lessened, but other factors can compensate to some extent.

Affirmative action, special skills or talents, unusual backgrounds, life experiences, evidence of strong perseverance or motivation, and strong LSAT scores can all overcome a relatively low UGPA.

On the other hand, an excellent UGPA alone does not guarantee your pick of the law school crop either. Because the LSAT score is usually weighted at least as heavily in the admissions calculus as UGPA and is considered by many to be a better and more objective predictor of law school success, many undergraduate academic stars are not accepted by the prestigious law schools of their choice. The LSAT is a standardized test specifically geared to test for the kinds of logic, comprehension, verbal, and analytical skills that prove helpful to the study of the law—skills that are not necessarily developed or encouraged by your undergraduate experience. The LSAT does not, however, test your drive, motivation, enthusiasm, or ability to memorize facts or learn over time.

Most law schools provide information about their current admissions standards in *The Official Guide to U.S. Law Schools: The Pre-Law Handbook,* which is published by the Association of American Law Schools. Given your LSAT score and UGPA, this information will allow you to make a reasonably accurate assessment of your chances of gaining admission to any given law school. The information also indicates, however, that intangible attributes play a major role once an applicant's scores place him within a certain range of acceptable candidates. The *Pre-Law Handbook* is a valuable resource and a must for the serious law school applicant.

The *Pre-Law Handbook* can be obtained, along with the *Information Book* (containing LSAT registration forms and information), by writing to LSAS (Law School Admissions Services), Box 2000, Newtown, PA 18940-0998. It is also available at many bookstores. Career guidance counselors at most universities and colleges will generally be able to give you a rough idea of which law schools you have a decent chance of getting into. Finally, you can also obtain information about admissions policies by writing directly to the admissions offices of the law schools that interest you.

The real secret to getting into the law school you want is to have a very high UGPA, a very high LSAT score, a very interesting and impressive personal statement, and glowing letters of reference from influential alumni who know you and your work well. Though few of us are so lucky, we can all make the best of the assets we do have.

Undergraduate Grade Point Average

Undergraduate grades are the product of a variety of factors, including intelligence, difficulty of major, and effort expended studying. By the time most people have decided to apply to law school, they are either already taking their college courses seriously and earning the best grades possible, or they are thinking of ways to minimize the adverse impact of relatively low grades.

If you are still in the early part of your college years and want to go to law school, do make every effort to get the best grades you can without depriving yourself of the joys of college life and the unique opportunities it presents. Also, take classes emphasizing writing and logical thinking, such as philosophy, English, rhetoric, and math. Such classes will develop skills that will be valuable throughout your law school studies.

Further, it cannot hurt your career options down the road to have taken engineering, chemistry, or biochemistry classes; intellectual property (for example, patents) and environmental law (for example, toxic torts) are currently hot areas of the law and will remain so in the foreseeable future. In light of the importance of Pacific Rim, Latin American, and European markets in our increasingly global economy, it is also definitely to your advantage to know a foreign language as well. Japanese, Mandarin, Cantonese, German, and Spanish, among other languages, could prove particularly helpful to a lawyer practicing in today's global marketplace.

Additionally, take classes that interest you, even if they do not seem related to your future legal career. Your interest in a class' subject matter will normally translate into better grades, which will advance your pursuit of a legal career.

The Law School Admission Test

Regardless of how you do in college or when you decide to go to law school, you can, and should, prepare thoroughly for the LSAT, a major criterion that is always within your control. As with any important test, the LSAT requires intense study and serious preparation. Though there may be exceptional individuals who can achieve high scores sitting for the test cold (that is, without studying), they are rare and you should not count on being one of them. Further, you may have been told that, since you can sit for the LSAT as many times as you wish, you can consider your first time taking the test as practice. Such an assertion is a harmful half-truth at best. Subsequent sittings can improve a poor first score. However, the first score will be averaged in with subsequent scores and the average score will be reported to law schools to which you apply. Thus, if you score a 150 on your first LSAT and an outstanding 170 on your second try, the average score will be only a modestly impressive 160. Most schools will use this average score in judging your admissions application. Therefore, like the bar exam, the LSAT is a test you should plan to take only once.

You can prepare for the LSAT by taking a formal lecture course, or by home study with the aid of a current test guide publication such as Harcourt Brace Jovanovich, Inc.'s *How To Prepare For The LSAT,* or ARCO's *LSAT.* With hard work, excellent results can be obtained with either method. Each method, however, has its own advantages.

A formal LSAT course offers individuals a structured method for preparing for the LSAT. Most of these courses have good instructors who have spent years studying the ins and outs of this exam and can impart at least some of their knowledge to their students. These courses can also offer their students realistic practice exams along with tips on the art of exam taking and timing. The best of the LSAT courses, and the one we recommend, is Stanley Kaplan's review course, which provides live lectures and taped analyses of old LSAT exams. While this preparation service is relatively expensive, a good LSAT score is worth the price, if you can afford it.

If you have the self-discipline to study without interruption on your own for three or four hours each day for several weeks, an equally good (and far less costly) method of LSAT study is by using a home study guide. One of us used such a method and achieved an LSAT score in the 94th percentile. If you choose this route, try to pick the most comprehensive and challenging study guide possible. Make sure it is updated and revised for the current LSAT format (the test format has changed significantly several times in the last 10 years). You should pace yourself and strictly follow the advice of the guide you have chosen; do not attempt to take a full-length exam at your first sitting since this will probably end up frustrating you. Because the LSAT is a timed test, you should take practice tests under timed conditions approximating actual exam conditions as closely as possible. If for any reason this is difficult for you to do on your own, you should strongly consider taking a formal review course.

Additionally, either method of studying for the LSAT can be supplemented by studying questions from previous tests. These old tests can be obtained from the Law School Data Assembly Service (LSDAS) for a nominal charge.

The LSAT score scale currently ranges from 120 to 180. The scoring system is *scaled*, meaning that your raw score (number of right answers) will be converted to a scaled score by applying a formula. The formula varies from test to test and is designed to adjust raw scores to account for varying degrees of difficulty between tests. The LSAT consists of five 35-minute sections, and a 30-minute writing sample is also required. The LSAT is a multiple-choice exam. Each 35-minute LSAT section presents a series of one type of multiple-choice questions. There are typically 22–28 questions in each series, and five answer choices are given for each question. One of the sections will be experimental and will not count toward your score, but you probably will not be able to tell which. You should therefore not even try to determine which section is experimental—just do your best on every section.

Course and home study guides analyze question types and classify them into groups such as reading comprehension, analytical reasoning (or logical games), and logical reasoning. These groups will correspond to the sections on the test itself. Since your LSAT score will be based solely on the number of correct answers you give, guessing is definitely advantageous.

The LSAT writing sample is a written essay in response to a previously unknown topic or question that is set forth at the end of the test. All that is required is a contemporaneous writing sample. There are no right or wrong essay answers—it is the quality and logical coherence of your prose and expositional skills that count. This part of the test is not reflected in your score, but it is sent to the law schools you apply to for evaluation.

Although it is not quantified as part of the LSAT score, the importance of the essay portion of the test should not be underestimated. While a good writing sample generally will not rescue a poor LSAT score, a poor writing sample may well undermine a good score. Some law schools also use the writing sample as a tiebreaker to decide between different students they are considering for a single spot in the incoming class. Improving your writing skills requires lots of practice, so take college courses that include frequent essay examinations. It also helps to read classics and other well-written literature. In addition, you should consult the classic text by Strunk and White, *The Elements of Style.*

The LSAT is given four times annually, in June, October, December, and February. You should set up a plan to study during the summer for the October exam; that way, if you need to, you can take the exam again in December and still be considered for admission to law school the following fall. You must register a month in advance of your test date to avoid paying a significant late registration fee. Registration materials and information can be obtained through your undergraduate college dean or pre-law advisor, or by writing to LSAS at the address given previously or calling LSAS at (215) 968-1001. You should also register for the LSDAS along with the LSAT. The LSDAS sends a report to all law schools you designate. The report includes:

- your LSAT score and writing sample
- a summary of your academic work
- your college transcript

Having LSDAS perform this essential service for you will ease your own work load during the stressful application process, and is now required by most law schools.

Letters of Recommendation and Other Materials

Besides your LSAT score and UGPA, law school admissions committees use application answers, writing samples, and letters of recommendation to evaluate candidates. Writing samples, in addition to the LSAT essay, are typically required by the law schools themselves. Most often, the law school requires you to write a personal statement, or an essay on a topic such as why you want to (or are uniquely qualified to) study law. These essays are very important and should be carefully crafted for both writing style and substance. They can go far toward making you stand out from other potential students in your UGPA/LSAT range.

Letters of recommendation are important, too. In securing such letters, you should be aware that letters written by individuals who are intimately familiar with your college work or other work habits almost universally carry the most weight. Thus, you should seek letters from former professors and employers who know something about you personally, rather than from famous alumni of the school you are applying to or other noteworthy individuals (unless, of course, such persons have personal knowledge of your analytical skills or work habits).

For example, if you did exceptionally well in a particular college course, ask the professor who taught the course to write you a letter of recommendation. Even if that professor does not remember you specifically, you can sit down with her and suggest that she could refresh her recollection about your talents by rereading an old exam or term paper. You may also provide her with your current résumé. Most professors who are approached in a courteous and respectful manner are flattered to be asked to write a letter of recommendation about their past students and will do so with a fair amount of thoughtfulness, skill, and accuracy.

The Application Process

Once you receive your LSAT scores and your letters of recommendation, you can determine your chances of getting into particular law schools by consulting the *Pre-Law Handbook* discussed previously. (Remember, though, that intangibles do enter into the mix.) Once you have ascertained your odds of getting into certain schools, plot a reasonable application strategy. Do not apply only to your "dream schools" where you know your chances of being accepted are slim. Otherwise you may well end up with no law school acceptances. Instead, cover all the bases by applying to a number of quality second-choice schools where your chances of acceptance are high. This way, you can still apply to a few dream schools that you desperately want to attend without feeling the intense pressure of having to beat the odds in order to go to law school at all.

Since the following chapter contains a detailed discussion of how to choose a law school, you should read it before submitting your applications. Note that being at least somewhat selective is important for most applicants, since law school application fees are not insubstantial and can run into hundreds of dollars or more if one takes a shotgun approach to the application process.

In submitting your applications, the following two suggestions can improve your chances of being accepted. First, be early. Get your applications in as soon as possible and pay attention to deadlines (which vary from school to school). Second, be complete. The materials that schools require vary somewhat, so be sure that you have included everything requested by the particular schools to which you are applying. A telephone call to each school's admissions office can answer any questions you may have regarding specific requirements.

A law school's selection process involves an admissions committee that includes professors who review individual student files, and each member of the committee may review literally thousands of applications. Some applicants are obvious "admits" and some are obvious "rejects," leaving a vast group in the "undecided" middle. Your goal is to make it as easy as possible for the committee to move you from the "undecided" group to the "admit" group.

Once your applications are submitted, you should wait alertly. Follow up promptly on any correspondence you receive from law school admissions offices. Since law schools have a difficult task in selecting students, they may want additional information, either as a matter of school policy or to learn more about a particular applicant. If the admissions office needs additional official transcripts from a college, promptly arrange to have them sent. If they want additional references, secure them immediately. It makes no sense to take the considerable time and effort to apply to a law school only to be rejected for a technical problem that easily could have been cured.

Some law schools require or at least provide opportunities for applicants to interview with alumni or school officials as part of the application process. A good interview can increase your chances of being accepted, so you should take advantage of such opportunities if geographically and economically feasible. Some schools accommodate geographically remote applicants by having alumni in the area conduct the interviews.

When you have diligently completed all of your applications and followed up on any related inquiries, sit down and relax. This may be difficult. Processing your application may take from a few weeks to several months, and this will seem like an endless period of time.

You may also receive a letter (as one author did from his first-choice school) informing you that you have been placed on a waiting list. This will delay the ultimate response even further. Being placed on a waiting list is not cause for despair, however, especially if it is at a law school you rate as a top choice. It simply means that you have survived the first round of cuts. A number of more-favored applicants have already received offers, and a number of less-favored applicants have already received rejections. You are in the middle; the law school would like to give you an offer to attend if its available places are not filled by its own first choices.

You can normally be assured that a number of more-favored applicants will decline any particular law school's offer of acceptance simply because they have been accepted at other schools they personally ranked higher. Remember, those hotshots with 4.0 GPAs and 175 LSATs have also wisely chosen schools where they are almost certain to be accepted as backups to their first choice. Their backup school, however, may be your dream school. In that case, you will just have to wait it out. (Incidentally, the author who was placed on a waiting list was offered and accepted admission to that first-choice school, just over a month before classes started. A fellow classmate even transferred to a different school, which accepted him during the first week of classes!)

Despite the general rule that you should not pester a law school's admissions office after your application is completed, there are some limited circumstances (in addition to those mentioned previously) where it might be appropriate for you to communicate with the school. This is especially true if you have been placed on the waiting list and there is additional material (such as a recent publication you have authored or award you have received) that you believe would positively influence your application if made known. The ultimate goal, after all, is to set yourself apart from your closest competitors and convince the admissions committee that you are a truly outstanding candidate.

The author who was placed on the waiting list submitted several free-lance newspaper articles he had written for the op-ed section of a major regional newspaper. While it is impossible to know for sure, perhaps those articles helped tip the balance in his favor. If you find yourself in similar circumstances, you should submit the additional material or information to the school as quickly as possible with a brief explanation as to why it was not sent earlier.

Once you have received responses from all the schools you applied to, you will hopefully be in a position to choose between at least several law schools. If so, act promptly and with consideration for the other people involved in the process. If you definitely know you will not be attending a school that has accepted you, inform the school promptly and courteously. If you desire to keep an acceptance open while waiting for a decision by your dream school, find out when the accepting school needs an answer from you, and inform it of your decision before the deadline. Once you have confirmed an acceptance, obtain and complete whatever additional paperwork is necessary to enroll. You may also request financial aid information and applications at this time.

This chapter was primarily devoted to providing information regarding admissions requirements and the application process for getting into law school. The next chapter is designed to help you choose wisely in making the very important and personal decision concerning which law school you wish to attend.

CHAPTER 3

Choosing a Law School that is Right for You: The Basic Considerations

"The difficulty in life is the choice."
— George Moore,
The Bending of the Bough, Act IV

The biggest key to enjoying law school is choosing and getting admitted to the right one for you. While there are 175 ABA-accredited law schools in this country, probably only a handful or so are optimal for you. Discovering this select handful of schools is the topic of this chapter.

There are really two logically distinct steps involved in choosing a law school: first, choosing the best schools to apply to, and second, choosing the law school you will attend from among those that have offered to admit you. You should consider yourself fortunate if you have any choice at all in the second regard given that many applicants, either as a result of poor application strategy or poor qualifications, do not receive offers of admission from any schools. (Consequently, as discussed in the previous chapter, it behooves you to make every effort to achieve a stellar academic record and to score as high as possible on the LSAT so as to increase your acceptance chances.) This chapter focuses primarily on choosing among schools that ultimately send you an acceptance letter. Since the application process also involves a ranking of schools on their relative merits, however, this chapter should also serve as a valuable guide with respect to which schools to apply to in the first place.

Besides your own "admitability," numerous other factors should be taken into account when deciding where to submit applications and ultimately which law schools to attend. These factors include:

- the national ranking or academic reputation of each school
- the geographic area in which you plan to practice law or live after law school
- the costs associated with attending the law schools in question
- the bar passage rates of such schools
- personal environmental and location preferences

Each of these factors is discussed as follows.

National Rankings and Academic Reputation

All things being equal, you should aspire to attend the most prestigious law school you can get into. While your choices will obviously be limited by your own credentials, choosing a law school with a good to excellent academic reputation (one of the top 40 or 50 law schools) will make you feel better about yourself and about your decision to attend law school. Also, top schools recruit the most talented faculty members and attract the brightest students. This contributes to a better legal education and a more intellectually stimulating and challenging experience. Such mental stimulation will help your law school years pass quickly.

Attending a law school with a good to excellent academic reputation also dramatically increases your chances of obtaining a prestigious and/or lucrative legal job following graduation. Top law firms and governmental agencies primarily recruit attorneys from the top law schools. The cream of the crop sought by employers is relative—the better the school, the less important the student's class ranking therein, and vice versa. The quality of your law school will continue to affect your career well after graduation and your first job. It will inform people's first impressions of you, and it will affect your ability to change jobs or obtain a new job in a different region of the country.

Further, your academic performance may be better in a school with an excellent academic reputation than in a mediocre law school. The advantages of having top faculty and students as catalysts for your own achievement should be obvious, but also the positive self-image fostered by matriculation at a better school can enhance your performance.

Additionally, some of the least prestigious law schools may attempt to bolster their standing by placing impossible demands upon their students and by flunking them out in droves to create the illusion that the school's academic standards are actually high. You should thoroughly investigate the academic reputation and prestige of each law school you are considering attending as well as its first-year attrition rate.

One way to assess the academic reputation associated with a school is by, among other things, checking the school's national ranking (if any) in published lists. Law schools are often ranked by various publications such as the *U.S. News and World Report.* These publications typically rate law schools according to the quality of their faculty, students, law libraries, general facilities, placement success, and curricula. Rankings in specialized areas such as tax law, clinical training, and environmental law are also often compiled.

Like any other subjective endeavor, law school rankings generate much debate as to their accuracy. However, for the most part, the same schools (for example, Yale, Harvard, Stanford, Chicago, and Columbia) are generally rated within the top five in the nation year in and year out. A number of other schools consistently appear in the top 20, top 25, or first quartile lists, though their exact positions vary with the particular evaluator or sources consulted. Law professors, judges, and lawyers may all have differing perspectives on which schools are the best. Thus, although the inherent imprecision of these rankings will enable debates to live on forever, there is probably a rough general consensus as to which law schools fall within the top 30 or 40 in terms of nationwide reputations for academic excellence.

In addition to national reputation and ranking, law schools also possess statewide and local reputations with regard to the level of professional training and academic excellence they offer. Local reputations can be gleaned from college career guidance counselors, lawyers, and law firms working in the community where the law school is located. Additionally, a law school's own admission standards are usually a good guide to its academic reputation. As a good rule of thumb, the less rigorous the admission standards, the less prestigious the law school, and vice versa. Look at the median LSAT scores and average UGPAs of applicants accepted at the schools you are interested in, and compare these to those of admittees at the schools ranked highly on a national level.

Geographic Area of Planned Practice

In deciding on which law school to attend, you should consider the geographical area where you hope to practice after graduation. There are several distinct advantages to attending a law school in or near your area of planned practice. Logistically, it will be easier to get both summer and permanent legal jobs in cities near your law school since most recruiters will probably be local and that is where the school's reputation is strongest. This is, of course, less true for very highly ranked law schools, because top law firm recruiters flock to such schools from all across the country. Even so, most law firms, particularly in recessionary times, recruit lawyers from law schools located relatively near them.

Another advantage to attending a law school near your area of planned practice is that it will offer courses (for example, community property) that may be of importance to practitioners in your state but are unavailable in other states.

Furthermore, by attending a law school in or near your area of planned practice, you can obtain valuable inside information from other students, local lawyers, and faculty members concerning what it is really like to work for various local and regional employers. You can clerk for such employers during your second and third years, earning money and valuable experience. The information thus gained can be used to avoid accepting an unsuitable job or to steer you toward employers who can offer you exciting career opportunities you might otherwise miss. Additionally, a large percentage of your classmates will be practicing in the area after graduation, providing opportunities to network during in your early years of practice.

Conversely, if you have no idea where you want to practice law, the importance of attending the most prestigious law school possible is greatly enhanced. The greater the prestige of your law school, the greater will be your opportunities to obtain legal employment anywhere in the country.

Other geographic factors to consider in selecting a law school are the accessibility to courts, government agencies, and legislatures, and the availability of part-time and summer jobs.

The Costs of Law School

Another important factor to consider is the economic cost associated with attending law school. Law school is a major financial investment.

Many potential law students fail to realize the importance of this factor, figuring they will somehow get by. This cavalier attitude toward the economic aspect of law school (or any graduate school for that matter) is a tremendous mistake. Unless you are independently wealthy or your parents are willing to pay for your law school education, costs are a highly significant (and often prohibitive) factor in selecting law schools. You simply do not want to be unduly worried about making ends meet throughout law school; obtaining a legal education is time-consuming and stressful enough in itself. You must be able to focus your energies while in law school on doing well without worrying about where your next rent check is coming from.

Begin your financial planning by considering whether your current savings or other available resources are sufficient to pay for your first year's tuition, books, food, housing, and living expenses at schools that interest you. If they are not, it is critical that you find out as early as possible what financial aid is available for each of the law schools you are considering attending. You should make this inquiry as early as possible because almost all financial aid programs have deadlines that must be met in order for you to be considered.

Additionally, many law school scholarships, which are available from or through individual law schools, must be applied for many months in advance of the start of the school year. For this reason, you should apply to the law schools you are interested in as early as possible. Each of your applications should include a request for information concerning financial aid from the school's admission office. Career guidance counselors at most colleges can also offer you valuable information about applying for financial aid for law school. Take advantage of their knowledge.

Cost considerations, while still important, are generally less of a concern during the second and third years of law school. This is because by then the options of well-paying legal jobs (full time in summer and part time during school) are more readily available than during the first year. However, a significant number of law schools are located in rural areas devoid of law firms and other legal employers needing law clerks. Thus, if the issue of finances concerns you, in addition to investigating the financial aid available, investigate what employment opportunities are available during the school year at the schools in question. Virtually all law schools have employment or placement offices staffed by full-time employees. These employees will normally be able to give you pertinent statistics concerning the availability of work during law school.

Finally, in evaluating a law school with respect to its costs, analyze the long-term costs and benefits. Consider not only the financial position attending that school will put you in for the next three years, but also the financial position it will put you in after you earn a degree and enter the legal marketplace. Compare the median starting salaries of graduates from the more expensive schools you are considering with those of graduates of the less expensive schools, along with the total expected debt from each. This comparison will give you an approximate idea of the relative financial benefits and burdens of attending each institution. Median and average starting salaries of graduates can be obtained from most law school employment or placement offices. You should also compare placement rates for graduates of the various schools while conducting this analysis.

Bar Passage Rates

This factor is obviously important. If you want to go to law school, you probably want to be a lawyer. This is impossible in most states, however, without passing a state bar examination (discussed in greater detail later). Accordingly, you should ascertain the bar passage rates of graduates of the schools you are considering attending. These figures are not guarantees, but they are very important statistics that are indicative of the quality of legal education of the school in question. Keep in mind that they are also subject to the usual individual variables of hard work and ability.

As one might expect, many times graduates from a particular school with good to average grades have, as a group, an excellent bar passage rate, but students from the same school with poor grades have, as a group, extremely low passage rates. You will not, of course, be able to further narrow your own odds until you attend a law school and fall into an identifiable GPA niche. However, the schools with the highest overall passage rates provide the highest comfort level to all groups. Not coincidentally, these schools also almost universally have good to excellent academic ratings. Therefore, all other criteria being equal, you should choose to attend a law school with a high bar passage rate.

Personal Environmental Factors

Just as important as the previous factors, and perhaps even more so, is that you attend a law school located in a region of the country that you like. Doing well in law school depends a great deal on your mental state. Consequently, if you pick a school that is perfect in all other respects but whose location or customary weather you absolutely hate, your law school performance will probably suffer. You may also be extremely unhappy during all three critical years of law school. Accordingly, in choosing schools, consider such things as:

- proximity to friends and family
- weather
- recreational and leisure opportunities
- the physical environment around the school (for example, is it located in an urban or suburban setting? Is it in the middle of a college campus? Is it by itself in a run-down area of a big city?)

Use common sense about your level of comfort with the physical environment of the school. For example, if you absolutely love going to the beach, think hard before saying yes to that excellent school in the midwest. If you love to ski every weekend, you probably will not want to study law in Hawaii.

The atmosphere of the school is another personal factor to be considered. Are relationships among students friendly or competitive? Are the professors friendly and accessible? How large are the first-year classes? How well your personality fits into the atmosphere of a place where you contemplate spending three years is an important consideration.

The best way to determine whether you like a school's setting, amenities, and surroundings is to visit that school. This should always be done before accepting an admission offer. Doing so will allow you to see where the law students live and determine whether the housing and living options available at or around the school suit you. It will also allow you to sit in on a few classes to see what the law school's faculty and students are like on a more personal level. The admissions office of the school in which you are interested can help you plan your visit. Call the admissions office and inform the staff that you are planning a visit. Ask the staff where to stay and if they would set up an informal meeting with some of the students at the school, as well as send you information on things to do in and around the school. Most admission offices will be happy to oblige and will work with you to make your visit a constructive one.

Visiting every school in which you are interested will normally be impossible due to monetary and time constraints. Thus, you may have to restrict your visits to the law schools that have offered you admission and that you are seriously considering attending. However, since personal environmental factors are absolutely crucial to your enjoyment of law school, it cannot be stressed enough that you should never decide to attend a law school without first visiting it.

Deciding what law school best suits you involves balancing numerous factors and gathering a great deal of information. Just as the law schools begin their selection of students many months before the next school year rolls around, you too should begin your selection process early. If you do so, you will probably end up choosing a law school that will give you an opportunity to have a successful and enjoyable three years. If not, you may unfortunately have a long, hard first year and a strong desire to attempt to transfer to a more agreeable law school environment for your second and third years.

Professional Publications, Inc. ▪ Belmont, CA

CHAPTER 4

Considerations Involved in Part-Time Law School Study

" 'Whom are you?' said he, for he had been to night school."
— George Ade, *Bang! Bang!*, "The Steel Box"

Of the 175 ABA-accredited law schools in this country, less than a quarter have part-time (late afternoon or evening) study programs leading to a JD degree. Generally, the schools that offer such programs are in the middle or on the lower end of the prestige scale and have less stringent admissions standards than the better schools. Still, for any number of reasons, a substantial number of law students in this country are enrolled in part-time school programs, and this book would not be complete without offering some advice to students in that situation.

Although the authors strongly recommend that any aspiring law student attempt to enroll in the full-time program of the best law school she can, there are a number of types of students who opt for part-time law study. Perhaps the student has a successful career and a well-paying job along with a family to support; in some cases, not enough financial aid will be available to enable the student to quit her present job and study full time. Perhaps the student wants to learn about the law to advance her present career without leaving her company's employment and does not wish to change careers following graduation from law school. Perhaps the student is an athlete in training, or for some other reason cannot study full time during the day. Or maybe the student simply prefers studying at night, the company of generally older, more mature students, and/or the lesser workload of a four-year part-time law school program. Whatever the reason a student is attending law school part time, however, there are a few pieces of sound advice to keep in mind.

The major obstacle to be overcome in order to succeed while studying law part time is the inherent lack of time available to the student. While most part-time law students consider the quality of the school's faculty and facilities, its costs, and its bar passage rate before deciding to attend (as they should), too few adequately envision the substantial compromises they will be forced to make because of time constraints. Almost all part-time law students work either part or full time. Many have demanding jobs and families to support. No matter how supportive the student's family is, there will inevitably be friction involved in the student's balancing of school, job, family, and recreation schedules. Often conflicts will arise at work, where the student's employer may view his law study in a negative light (as simply a "ticket out" from his present job). For example, such employers will tend not to understand that the student is unable or unwilling to make that important and time-consuming business trip because of his law studies.

Many part-time law students get very little sleep. Most have the sense that each part of their lives—school, job, and family—are compromised to some extent by their situation. If they are able to sleep only four or five hours per night, their minds are not fresh for study or work, and they may be irritable and short with family members. If they spend too much time with their families, they will be unable to complete their law assignments, and may fall behind, with a consequent diminution in their academic performance. If they excel in their jobs, they may have no time or energy left for family or law school. Rather than being able to develop any comfortable routine, part-time law students must often study whenever they can in a "catch as catch can" manner, often studying on weekends and at odd hours.

Throughout their studies, part-time law students must sometimes be prepared to deal with the negative feelings employers and families often have about their studies, as well as criticism from their professors for not keeping current on their assignments. Accordingly, in order to successfully effect (to the extent possible) the difficult balancing act that will be required, the student should sit down with those affected— employers and family members—before undertaking a part-time law study program in order to completely explain the course of action she is going to undertake. While this may not be easy, it is critical to enlist the support of these important people from the start to avoid future conflicts. The part-time law student will experience enough stress without adding fractured relationships caused by poor or incomplete communication.

It is also important for the part-time student to develop a rapport with his professors that will establish the necessary flexibility with respect to the student's ability to attend classes. If work or family conflicts make regular attendance difficult, let your professor know what is going on and what you are doing to make up for the classes missed. Most law professors are reasonable persons and will understand the rigorous demands the part-time law student is placing upon himself and others in his life.

Aside from realizing beforehand the severity of the time constraints involved, the necessity for a skillful balancing of many areas of the part-time student's life, and the unhappy reality that success or performance in many of these areas will almost inevitably be compromised, the principles of studying law part time are no different than would otherwise be the case. Obviously, options such as moot court, law review, and judicial clerkships and externships will almost certainly be unworkable, but the principles of briefing, using study aids, outlining, and preparing for examinations discussed elsewhere in this book still apply. Thus, although part-time law study is not a preferred option, knowing what to expect and dealing with it as directly and honestly as possible will help the student make the best of the situation.

Professional Publications, Inc. ▪ Belmont, CA

A Basic Law School Primer

Chapter 5: The First Year of Law School:
             Debunking the Myth

Chapter 6: Study Aids:
             The Dos and Don'ts of Outside Reading

Chapter 7: Studying for and Taking Law School Exams

Chapter 8: Choosing Second- and Third-Year Courses

The First Year of Law School: Debunking the Myth

"...out of the midst of the fire, of the cloud, and of the thick of darkness."

— Deuteronomy, Ch. V

The first year of law school is the stuff of myths and legends, hyperbole and dramatic portrayals in both books and movies. It is the best of times and the worst of times, that wonderful, harrowing year of intellectual transformation and academic purgatory into which you naively stride with a "skull full of mush" and out of which you emerge (if you survive) "thinking like a lawyer"—obviously the ultimate virtue!

Faced with the daunting myth of the first year, it is not surprising that most law students dread starting law school. They believe that their own Professor Kingsfield, that pedantic tyrant of first-year contracts from *The Paper Chase,* lurks inside each new classroom they enter. This is simply untrue. The first year is difficult for most students mainly because it presents a new and unknown challenge. By contrast, the curriculum in the second and third years of law school is much harder than that offered in the first year, and the workload is twice as great. The stress and difficulty associated with taking the bar exam far exceeds that associated with the dreaded first-year exams. And appearing before a cantankerous judge with a real client's rights and money—perhaps even his freedom—on the line is clearly a much tougher task than fielding a few questions from any first-year professor. Yet the myth of the first year as some mysterious and unknowable transforming experience persists, to the detriment of many students.

Professional Publications, Inc. • Belmont, CA

The first year, while not wholly deserving of the mythic stature the media and others seem to have conferred upon it, is nevertheless very important. How well you do in your first-year classes in terms of grades disproportionately affects your ability to get choice summer, and even permanent, law-related jobs. In fact, first-year grades are usually far more important than second- and third-year grades, since your prospective employers often will have made their decisions about you before the latter grades are made available. The trick, then, is to take the first year of law school seriously and realize its importance, but not to be overwhelmed by it. Having a good idea about what to expect before you start will help debunk the first-year myth, eliminate needless anxiety, and reduce stress to a manageable level, allowing you to achieve the best grades you can.

This chapter begins to debunk the myth by introducing you to the classes you will most likely take during your first year, the types of fellow students you will meet, and the types of professors you can expect. It also includes a section on the numerous study aids that you will encounter during your first year of law school (the supplemental reading materials designed to help you better understand and master the principles of law taught in your substantive courses). This chapter and the next (on studying for and taking law school exams) contain the first rules and instructions for playing the law school game.

The first rule is that eliminating unpleasant surprises—the kind promoted by the first-year myth—will greatly enhance your performance. You can avoid many of these unpleasant surprises by being prepared when school starts. The following table lists the items that the first-year law student should obtain before the first day of class or shortly thereafter.

Essential	Recommended
assortment of pens and highlighters	computer
tape recorder	printer for computer
Black's Law Dictionary	word-processing program
plenty of 11″ × 14″ legal pads for taking notes	cookbook containing recipes for easy and quick meals
casebooks and other assigned reading materials	
commercial outlines for assigned courses (excluding legal research and writing)	

By debunking the myth and setting forth fundamental rules and information about first-year classes, fellow students, and professors, this chapter and the next are aimed at making your first year of law school much more like everyone else's second year.

First-Year Classes: What to Expect

First-year classes are assigned and scheduled for you. There are no electives in the first year. In addition, first-year students are generally assigned to sections, so that you will see the same people in virtually all your first-year classes.

First-year courses are designed not only to impart substantive knowledge about general areas of the law, but also to teach students how to think like a lawyer. Many laypeople believe that the law is a vast collection of specific rules that dictate the correct outcome for every imaginable set of facts. First-year courses are designed to disabuse the neophyte of such notions, because facts are infinitely variable and the rules cannot provide for every possible combination.

First-year students are introduced to the *case study* method of learning. Under this method, students study cases in which specific sets of facts give rise to specific results, and they discuss whether changing certain facts should or should not lead to different results.

Following are law school classes you are likely to have during your first year of law school along with brief comments about each class.

Contracts

Contracts is the study of "deals"; it is the study of how binding and legally enforceable agreements are reached in our society and what happens when such agreements are *breached,* or not performed according to their terms. Without the "commercial glue" of contracts, our society's economy could not function. A free-market economy depends to a large degree on people being able to rely on others to perform their solemn promises as specified in their deals.

The law of contracts is vast, and the variety of factual settings in which disputes arise is infinite. Many contract professors unfortunately (but in keeping with the first-year myth) tend to overwhelm their students with too much factual detail and relatively insignificant garble. To combat this tendency, students need to focus on the big picture (that is, how contracts are formed and breached, types of breaches, defenses to a claim of breach or nonperformance, and rudimentary contractual damage measurements or principles). Other topics discussed in class may deserve much less emphasis than they in fact receive, and students should try to keep sight of the forest amidst all the trees. The basic idea is that promises people make are enforceable when certain rules are followed and certain conditions are met.

Property

Most first-year property classes deal with the creation, transfer, and ownership of rights in *personal property* (that is, movable things and intangibles, like notes and contract rights) and *real property* (land and fixtures attached thereto). For reasons that are unclear (but again in keeping with the first-year myth), too much class time is usually devoted to the confusing study of archaic real property rules (that is, future interests and estates) created in the Middle Ages. What your professor will probably not tell you is that very little of such discussions is relevant in modern practice or often even at exam time. Much of this material is very boring to everybody except your property professor. As a result, unless you are one of those students with a natural affinity for property law, you may be left with the formidable task of trying to stay awake in enough classes so that you can figure out what areas might actually appear on your exam.

Fortunately, however, property classes are not all about archaic rules and hypotheticals concerning "Blackacre." Issues stemming from land-lord/tenant disputes, secured transactions, land use and takings, and environmental law are often very interesting and of tremendous current relevance and significance. This is an area of the law characterized by the opposing forces of development, on the one hand, and preservation and growth limitations, on the other. Property law is the battlefield on which this conflict will be fought.

In any event, reviewing old exams given by your property professor can be of significant value in getting a grasp on this course. Such a review should at least indicate what material your property professor really feels is important.

Torts

Torts is the study of noncontractual legal theories by which people can obtain compensation for injuries to their persons or property resulting from the wrongful conduct of another. Torts professors are famous for discussing incredibly bizarre hypothetical questions in class, such as whether Mr. X should be liable for all damages occurring as a result of his lighting a match in a restaurant's nonsmoking section when he did not know the restaurant was filled with explosive gas as a result of a negligently repaired leak. The gas exploded when the match was lit, causing the building to shake and resulting in a seismically unsafe sign over the entrance falling on top of Mr. Y, who was swinging from it as part of his Tarzan imitation at the time and who is now suing Mr. X for the ruination of his sex life, among other things.

During the first part of the year, torts class is generally devoted to *intentional torts* (like battery, assault, trespass to land and chattels, conversion, and false imprisonment) as well as the vague and perplexing tort of *negligence* (essentially, unreasonable conduct that foreseeably causes another to suffer unintended harm or injury). A common element of torts is that the persons committing them (called the *tortfeasors*) are at fault for some reason.

During the second part of the year, *strict liability torts* are usually examined. Under such torts, an entity (such as a manufacturer of products or conductor of ultrahazardous activities) or person is deemed liable for injuries caused by product defects or as a result of his or her conduct, even if the conduct was reasonable and performed with due care, for reasons of public policy and regardless of fault. The defendant's exercise of due care is thus deemed irrelevant to the determination of liability when rules of strict or absolute liability apply.

As proven by lawyers such as San Francisco's flamboyant Melvin Belli (the so-called "King of Torts"), tort law is certainly colorful and sometimes quite lucrative. Class discussions evoke mental pictures of ambulance chasers, exploding soda bottles, mischievous children, airplane crashes, and neighborhood fender benders, and of huge jury verdicts and contingent fees. With the possible exception of criminal law, tort law is probably the one area of study that most laypeople associate with lawyers. For this reason, most law students pay attention and enjoy this class, and consider it to possess some sort of intrinsic value as the real "stuff" of lawyering.

Criminal Law

There is little that is uplifting about studying the various degrees of murder or other crimes, especially when they may not make sense to your pre-law school notions of justice. For example, you may question why a person who plans for just a few hours to kill a violent person who previously provoked him should get a stiffer sentence than a person who simply goes berserk one day and slashes to death the little old lady down the street by stabbing her 1,000 times in a random fashion. But the law, in its dispassionate, reasoned fashion, says such is the case. Under the law, the *mens rea* (state of mind) involved in planning a murder is more culpable than that associated with a fit of rage or insanity, even though the *actus reus* (the act) in all homicide cases has the same end result.

Much of the criminal law taught in law school is devoted to studying the different types of murder (premeditated, depraved-heart, felony murder, etc.). Depending on the professor's individual predilections, less morbid crimes such as burglary, embezzlement, theft, robbery, arson, assault, mayhem, and kidnapping may take the spotlight or may scarcely be touched upon. A balanced approach will be employed if you are lucky enough to have a criminal law professor who realizes that some students still actually go into this area of practice and that all lawyers need a basic grounding in criminal law, if for no other reason than to understand just how delicate and tenuous the basic nature of our guarantees of personal liberty can be.

Civil Procedure

This class is about judicial power and how it is invoked in the cause of justice. Here the student will learn how certain courts obtain power, or *jurisdiction,* over individuals and organizations *(personal jurisdiction)*; civil procedure class also addresses the types of issues various courts are competent to decide *(subject matter jurisdiction)*. More mundane matters covered by this class include the effects of a court's judgments and orders on subsequent lawsuits *(res judicata* or *collateral estoppel)*. The course also explores the technical and highly complex rules that must be followed to properly bring cases before a court; typical forms of investigating facts, or *discovery* (for example, depositions, document requests, and interrogatories); and other selected rules of state and federal procedure, such as those governing *class actions* (lawsuits where large numbers of individuals can benefit from or be bound by a judgment even though they are not actually named parties to the lawsuit).

Because of its initially confusing terminology and its rather dry and technical nature, civil procedure often causes a lot of trouble for first-year law students. Cognizant of this fact, some schools defer teaching the class until the second year, when the more mature students' greater acclimation to the legal environment allows them to more readily absorb the dry and dense maze of procedural and jurisdictional rules.

Additionally, some schools have begun integrating practical aspects of practicing law into the civil procedure course. These aspects include activities like interviewing "clients" and deposing "witnesses."

Constitutional Law

Because the subject matter of constitutional law is so vast, it is usually covered in two or three courses, one of which may be taken during the first year of study. Major aspects of this area of legal study include the First Amendment (freedom of speech and association), the Fourth Amendment (prohibition against unreasonable searches and seizures), the Fifth Amendment (right to due process and prohibition against involuntary self-incrimination), the Fourteenth Amendment (equal protection), and the Commerce Clause, which gives the federal government its enormous power to regulate just about whatever activity it wants.

Constitutional law classes tend to generate lively and entertaining debate among both students and professors. This area of study brings to the forefront such controversial issues as the right to abortion and the constitutional safeguards afforded those accused of crimes in this country (the infamous media-designated "technicalities"), such as the rule excluding evidence obtained by illegal searches.

Legal Research and Writing

With regard to perceived importance, this is probably the most underrated first-year course. However, in terms of helping you write legal memoranda and briefs during your summer legal jobs and future employment, this is the most important class you will take. In this class, you will learn the fundamentals of searching for the law, skills that you will employ throughout your legal career. The law is found in the U.S. Constitution (the "Supreme Law" of our country), treaties, federal statutes (passed by Congress), state constitutions (supreme within the sphere of state law), state statutes (passed by state legislatures), the Federal Rules of Civil Procedure (judicially made rules governing civil practice in federal courts), state court rules (statewide and local), local ordinances, published federal and state case decisions (containing the "common law," that is, judge-made law in nonstatutory areas), and various other more obscure hiding places.

The belief held by many laypersons that any attorney knows the law "off the top of his head" is wrong. While many skilled practitioners do know a lot of law (or, more accurately, are readily familiar with its general substance and where to find it), especially in the areas they specialize in, a simple tour of a decent law library would easily demonstrate that no one could memorize even a fraction of the written law in this country. As a lawyer, you must know how to search for the law because it is too complex, massive, and ever-changing to commit it all to memory. Teaching you how to find the applicable law comprises the research portion of your legal research and writing course. You will learn to conduct legal research the "old-fashioned" way by finding and reading written texts and also by using the computer data base systems of LEXIS and WestLaw.

Aside from teaching basic research skills, a research and writing class should also impart the basic tenets of legal writing. Generally, a modern lawyer is only as effective as the words and arguments she can put in her briefs.

Unfortunately, legal research and writing classes are often taught by people barely out of law school themselves (and sometimes by second- or third-year assistants who are not yet out of law school). Although teaching these important classes is difficult and very time-consuming, the job of legal research and writing instructor is invariably at the very low end of law school teaching positions both in terms of prestige and remuneration.

To make matters worse, many law schools (foolishly, in our view) do not give standard letter grades for this class. Consequently, many first-year law students tend to discount the importance of this class and pay only minimum attention to its subject matter. This is a serious mistake that has recently been manifesting itself in complaints from top law firms that their young recruits lack even the most basic research skills. Put simply, you cannot know or use the law if you cannot find it. To find it, you need to be familiar with the nature and location of the law's sources. Furthermore, writing ability is equally important, since even if you can find the law and learn it, you will be unable to use it effectively if you are incapable of writing well.

If you do not take your legal research and writing class seriously, you may well end up embarrassing yourself at your first legal job when you are asked (as you no doubt will be) to research a legal issue of some import to your employer. This type of embarrassment is something most aspiring lawyers (and their employers) want to avoid. Hence, a good rule of thumb for this class is to spend no less time proportionately on it than on any other class you are taking your first year. The hours spent laying a sound research and writing foundation will pay significant dividends on your initial investment of time.

First-Year Professors: What to Expect

The initial exposure of first-year law students to professors can be intimidating. As with all other aspects of law school, and the first year in particular, knowing what to expect ahead of time should decrease your anxiety and improve your performance.

The Socratic Method

It is widely, though erroneously, believed that all law school professors are intimidating Professor Kingsfield-types who employ the Socratic method of teaching. The so-called *Socratic method* refers to a method of teaching by which the professor elicits the information he desires to impart to the class primarily by questioning, not lecturing. In addition to imparting information, the goal of the Socratic method is to teach students how to think critically about issues.

The name of the method is derived from the ancient Greek philosopher Socrates' habit of persistently questioning his fellow Athenians to demonstrate the actual extent and limits of their knowledge. While in years past most law school professors employed the Socratic method of teaching by questioning, that method has been much criticized (especially by students). In our experience, modern law professors use the Socratic method to a lesser degree.

Still, there are many die-hard Socratic professors remaining. These professors' stern demeanors and constant interrogations can be quite intimidating to first-year law students who have never before experienced this teaching method. It is bad enough to have to wade through dozens of pages of incomprehensible legalese before coming to class utterly confused; it is far worse to then have your confusion compounded by merciless interrogation by a professor who has read the assigned cases hundreds of times and who will not accept "pass" for an answer. Throw in the additional fear of being exposed as an inarticulate intellectual weakling in front of your peers—a room full of stellar academics you already misperceive as being brighter than you—and you begin to get the picture of how truly intimidating the Socratic method can be.

The ways to combat your fear of the Socratic method are simple. The first rule is to always come fully prepared to the Socratic professor's class. This means you need to thoroughly read the assigned cases and adequately brief them. Be prepared to recite the facts of the cases in a short, pithy manner (ideally, verbatim from your brief) if called upon to do so.

Further, be prepared to state and defend your reading of a case's holding and rationale against an onslaught of questions that are designed to try to move you from your initial position.

Finally, be prepared to discuss the significance of the case and where the law might go next, or how the holding might be extended to differing factual situations. Do not be afraid to disagree with your professor in a firm but polite manner, as long as you have well-supported, logical reasons for doing so. Even if your position is wrong (which it may well not be if the professor is simply playing devil's advocate), your professor will respect you if you have presented an articulate and reasoned defense of it. Furthermore, there are no right or wrong answers to many questions the Socratic professor asks, only arguments for different results; therefore, do not hesitate to defend a position even if you are not completely convinced it is correct. After all, as a practicing lawyer, you will be called upon to argue both strong and weak legal positions, and this is as good a time as any to begin training.

Additionally, it helps to look at the exercise from the professor's viewpoint. Teaching students to think like lawyers is at least as important as imparting knowledge of the substantive legal rules. Cases in the casebooks show how the legal rules are applied to specific facts, and these examples are the building blocks for class discussion. The professor wants students to be able to ascertain what facts are important to the result, and how the result might change if certain facts are changed. The final exam will test your ability to apply the legal rules to a factual situation you have never seen before. Of course, that is what lawyers do every day. Thinking like a lawyer also encompasses thinking about why the law is the way it is and how or why it might change. The professor's questions are designed to engage you in this way of thinking, not to elicit memorized responses.

While it may be difficult to remain calm when called upon by a Socratic professor, make every effort to do so. Realize that all other students in your class are in the same boat as you and are equally subject to being called on and perhaps embarrassed. You should find that they realize this too, and are hence respectful of their classmates' efforts in the hope that they will receive similar support and sympathy when their turns come. Do not be intimidated. Reaffirm to yourself that you are just as capable and bright as any of your classmates. Consider the professor's questions a challenge, and do not be afraid to rise to meet it (sometimes literally, in the case of those professors who require their students to stand when called upon).

Finally, if you are caught in the unenviable position of being unprepared for the Socratic professor's questions, having not done the assigned reading, your professor will probably appreciate it if you would just tell him the truth. You should also briefly explain the extenuating circumstances that prevented your preparation, and allow him to shift the questioning to other, prepared students. If this occurs, you will have made the most of the situation by virtue of your honesty, and you will have not wasted the professor's and your classmates' time by trying to bluff your way through an oral examination you are destined to fail. Be aware, however, that the professor will return to question you during the next class, not only to determine whether you have done the assigned reading (or have a habit of not doing so), but also to fairly distribute the workload of his Socratic questioning.

In short, Socratic professors are not to be feared, but are to be respected and considered merely another of law school's many challenges.

Other Teaching Methods

Socratic professors are not the only type of professor (or even most common type of professor) you will be dealing with in law school. Some professors primarily lecture, while others use modern techniques such as problem solving, simulations, or role playing. Many professors use a combination of methods, including some Socratic aspects, while attempting to be less intimidating.

Other professors, while not Socratic, are equally strict in their proscriptions of tardy arrivals and inappropriate classroom demeanor (for example, making noise, talking, chewing gum, etc.). Such professors, at their best, are compulsive with respect to the organization of their lecture presentations, as well as the punctiliousness of their students.

Careful, accurate notes should be taken in their classes, for lectures by this type of fastidious professor are often the most valuable in terms of clarity and comprehensiveness. Their students are rewarded simply for attending class and taking good notes.

Still other professors may not present carefully organized lectures in a note-taking sense, but nevertheless give such a lively and interesting presentation that the class cannot help but be enthralled. Such professors may leap about the class, raising and lowering the intonation of their voices, and illustrating their lectures with loud claps and wild hand movements. These professors are like professional thespians, and they put on quite a show. Class participation in such classes comes naturally and enthusiastically, unlike in the classes of some other professors. Do not mistake the showman professor's entertaining classroom behavior for a lack of academic standards, however, or you may be unpleasantly surprised at test time. Prepare for his class just as much as everyone else's.

Other types of professors include the distinguished scholar but not-so-good-teacher, the excellent-student-just-turned-inexperienced professor, and the accomplished practitioner devoting some time to teaching law (often one of the very best types of professors). A good general rule is to treat all professors with respect and to give them all the professional courtesy of preparing for their classes thoroughly. They will appreciate this, and it is to your advantage as well. Also, try not to pester your professors by phone during their off-hours with constant questions; rather, attend their scheduled office hours and present your questions in a clear, articulate, and logically organized fashion after you have made a reasonable effort to ascertain the answers on your own.

Finally, it cannot be stressed enough that you should not be intimidated by your professors. While your professors are lawyers with elite academic credentials and legal abilities far superior to your own (at present), this should not make you feel inadequate, since they have obviously been at it for many more years than you have. In the final analysis, realize that your professors are there to help you learn, and they should be viewed as resources, not enemies.

First-Year Classmates: What to Expect

A discussion of first-year personalities would not be complete without mention of your fellow students and the various impacts they may have on you. Learning what to expect from them should not be part of a plot to undermine their efforts and exploit their weaknesses in a competitive manner. Rather, it is simply a way to preserve your own psychological health. Why is this so? Generally, your fellow law students were very successful undergraduates. By and large, they majored in the humanities or liberal arts. The majority came directly to law school from college, although there is a growing number of older students going back to school after raising a family or moving on from another career. Most law students are normal people of above-average intelligence, and they are witty and fun to be around. However, a few personality types are either so compulsive or competitive that they cannot help (whether intentionally or unintentionally) undermining your own confidence and mental well-being by making you question your own abilities.

A simple rule is to avoid, if at all possible, personality types that make you anxious and nervous. Some students will claim to study 24 hours a day and talk about nothing but law. Although their claims of great scholarship are of dubious validity, these types can nevertheless make you question whether what you are doing is adequate, even though you are fully prepared and studying as hard as you reasonably can. It is better to avoid these types entirely unless you can limit your contacts to mutually helpful arrangements involving note-sharing and other activities of reciprocal benefit (a doubtful proposition). You simply do not need the extra stress of worrying about whether you should be losing sleep doing unassigned reading. If you do a good job on the assigned reading and make judicious use of appropriate study aids, you need not worry about whether you are studying enough.

Another type of law student to avoid is the type that drains you emotionally by making constant unreciprocated demands for time, notes, briefs, study materials, outlines, etc. Often these students do not go to class themselves; when they do, their notes are poor or nonexistent, and they are unable to discuss the pertinent concepts and issues intelligently. Whether they are simply lazy or not, it does not behoove you to enter into a time-consuming relationship with individuals who will always take and never give. While you can, and should, have mutually beneficial arrangements with many other law students (with respect to tape-recording missed classes, providing copies of notes, and discussing issues), you should make sure that you are getting something out of such relationships as well. After all, you are attending law school to obtain your own legal education, not to educate someone else in a way that detracts from your primary goal. Additionally, you do not need the psychological headache of feeling like you have been taken advantage of. This will produce negative emotional responses that impede your ability to absorb the course material and prepare for examinations.

Another type of student with whom you may have an unsettling encounter is the man or woman who, while never seeming to study, claims to be getting stellar grades. The danger here is you may be tempted to emulate what you believe this person is doing by underpreparing for your classes and exams. "If," the devil on your right shoulder may be saying to you, "this person is going to ball games, on ski trips, and out to nightclubs and bars on a daily basis and still getting good grades, why can't I?" There are two answers. First, if the individual in question really is succeeding academically with minimal preparation, she is probably brilliant, and your law school career is too important to gamble on finding out whether you are just as brilliant. Second, the distinct possibility exists that you are being misinformed and the individual is not actually doing as well as she reports. In either case, your study strategy should not change one iota.

Lastly, you may encounter fellow students with strongly held political, religious, or philosophical viewpoints who mistakenly believe law school is a debating forum and that political rhetoric is an acceptable mode of legal analysis. Be assured that it is not. At exam time, most of your professors will be looking for legal rules and some logical application of these rules to the facts your exam presents. Political rhetoric will rarely, if ever, get you any credit, either in law school (with the possible exception of a legal philosophy class known as Critical Legal Studies) or in the courts. Therefore, while it may be tolerated by lenient or bored first-year professors, it is best to just ignore much of the babbling that inevitably spews forth in all first-year classes. Concentrate instead on what the cases say and what the professor says and asks.

With the foregoing in mind, you should have at least a fairly good idea of what to expect from your first-year law professors and fellow students. Remember, knowing what to expect ahead of time and avoiding unpleasant surprises is a big part of becoming acclimated as quickly as possible to the law school environment and scoring as high as you can in the law school game.

CHAPTER 6

Study Aids:
The Dos and Don'ts of Outside Reading

"A learned fool is one who has read everything,
and simply remembered it."

— Josh Billings, American Humorist

One reason law school is unique is because it is the only school where a student can make a conscious effort to avoid attending a class, yet end up scoring higher on the final exam than many of her fellow students who laboriously attended and prepared for every lecture. (However, while this is possible in law school, it is not recommended.)

The reason for this curious phenomenon is simple: many law students do not know how to play the law school game. Contrary to what your professors may tell you, an integral part of playing the law school game is the judicious use of study aids. What are law school study aids? In brief, they are straightforward sources of "the law"—those legals rules and principles that are crucial for you to know at test time.

As an initial matter, you should accept the fact that you, too, will buy and use commercial study aids even after you have spent a bundle just to attend law school and purchase the required texts. There are several reasons you will do so. The primary reason is to clarify and organize the mass of unfamiliar materials you will be studying. Both law school professors and the textbooks they use tend to obscure the so-called "black letter" law you need to know to get good grades within a massive exposition of text, ideas, and questions. Unlike the judicial opinions found in the casebooks (which will be your primary sources of assigned reading), law school study aids contain straightforward statements of black letter law, its sources, and its rationales, along with a few illustrations of its application. Thus, they help to unobscure the obscure. Accordingly, they will enable you to spend considerably less time organizing and learning a subject than would otherwise be necessary.

In addition to helping you make the most efficient use of your study time, such aids (when used wisely) free up time for enjoying those activities that are not necessarily associated with being a law student. Also, since the majority of your fellow students will be using study aids, you may be at a competitive disadvantage if you do not do the same.

This chapter provides the new law student with an overview of the various types of study aids available, including advice on how and when to use them and which ones to use. We hope this will help reduce some of the anxiety engendered by the existence and variety of these materials.

Part of the wise use of study aids is knowing when and how not to use them. Study aids, like alcohol, should be used in moderation. You should not rely upon them exclusively to learn the subject matter of your classes. Overreliance on or addiction to study aids can make you intellectually lazy and can hamper the development of your ability to read and analyze case law for its salient points, an essential skill for any lawyer. This chapter therefore concludes with some appropriate caveats aimed at preventing a student from becoming addicted to study aids or from otherwise using them in a harmful fashion.

The Existing Hodgepodge of Study Aids

Commercial Outlines

Of the many types of study aids, the most commonly used is the commercial outline. *Commercial outlines* are published summaries of specific areas of the law (for example, torts, contracts, or criminal law) prepared exclusively for law students by law professors and other individuals with legal backgrounds. Their great advantage is that they give the law student the basic points of law needed to master a subject for exam-taking purposes in one highly condensed and relatively compact source. They also illustrate coherent ways to organize your own personal outlines.

As explained in more detail in the chapter on studying for and taking law school exams, commercial outlines should be used not as a substitute for, but rather as a supplement to, your own personal course outlines. They are also useful for a review of the basic points of a course, both during its initial stages and immediately prior to exams—especially when you are having trouble mastering or understanding particular material. Most commercial outlines also contain sample exam questions and answers that can fruitfully be used to practice exam writing and analysis skills.

A number of companies publish commercial outlines, but in our experience the best outlines are consistently marketed under the names of *Gilbert Law Summaries* and *Emanuel Law Outlines*. While both are excellent, the differences between the two are marked. The Gilbert outlines are written, under the auspices of a board of editors comprised of dozens of top law school faculty members from across the country, in a traditional bare-bones outline form. They are relatively short and are packed with terse statements of the law with citation to its sources, but they offer less in-depth explanation of concepts at issue than do Emanuel's outlines. By contrast, Emanuel's outlines, written by 1976 Harvard Law School graduate Steven Emanuel, look and read more like novels (though admittedly ones not packed with excitement and suspense).

Another difference is in the number of different course topics covered. Gilbert outlines cover a broader spectrum of courses, including many second- and third-year courses. Emanuel outlines cover a more limited selection of courses and maintain a particularly good reputation with respect to their treatment of first-year classes.

Which brand or type of outlines you use is generally a matter of personal preference, availability, and need. However, in selecting a commercial outline, it makes sense to consider the following:

- An outline written or edited by the professor teaching your course (or by a professor who wrote the textbook you are using) will usually be more helpful than other outlines covering your course topic.

- An outline written by a noted expert in the field is often better than its competitors.

- "Tried and true" outlines recommended by trusted fellow students for a particular course or professor are often superior to outlines not so recommended.

We can recommend the following outlines based on our experiences and those of our fellow law students:

- Emanuel for contracts, criminal law, and criminal procedure and property
- *Gilbert Law Summaries* for torts and real property
- Sum & Substance's civil procedure outline

Unfortunately, commercial outlines, like most law school study aids, are outrageously priced. If you are strapped for money, consider sharing commercial outlines with equally impecunious classmates, rotating on a scheduled basis. Fortunately, law libraries often carry a limited number of such outlines for student use. Used outlines may also be obtained either for free or at a fraction of their original cost from other law students who have already taken the particular class.

Bar Outlines

Bar outlines, as their name implies, are commercial outlines designed to help law school graduates prepare for the bar exam. Students can use such outlines to study for law school classes, since they essentially impart the same black letter law as commercial outlines.

Law students can obtain bar outlines when they sign up for a bar review course, which they can do at any time. Because such courses are expensive, most students usually do not sign up for a review course until nearly the end of law school; thus they lack access to bar outlines until such time. Some bar review courses allow students to sign up for their services during the first and second years of law school for only a small down payment on the total price. (They also usually offer a small discount on the total price for an earlier sign-up.) They then provide such students with copies of their bar outlines at little or no extra cost to assist them with their law school classes.

Because they are written as refreshers for those who have already struggled with and learned the key rules and concepts, bar outlines tend to be sketchier and contain fewer helpful illustrations and hypotheticals than commercial outlines. For this reason, the authors do not believe bar outlines are particularly helpful study aids for most law students.

Fellow Law Student Outlines

Invaluable, but frequently overlooked or underutilized, sources of helpful outlines are your fellow students. The outlines of top students, especially those who have gotten A's in the particular class, are often outstanding, and copies are sometimes still being circulated years after the student has graduated. Such outlines can be obtained in a variety of ways—from the authors themselves, from your friends, or on a *quid pro quo* basis from other students. Be ever alert for an opportunity to obtain a copy of the outline of the student who *Am Jur'ed* (that is, got the highest A and thus received an award from the publisher of the *American Jurisprudence* treatise) in property or contracts the previous year. Such an outline will likely be more valuable than any commercial outline on the subject—especially if you have the same professor the author did, since the outline will then be specifically tailored to your own professor's predilections, idiosyncrasies, and biases.

Likewise, if you know one of your classmates is at the top of your class and does a thorough job of outlining, see if you can study with him and obtain a copy of his outline, perhaps offering to share your own outlines, class notes, and other materials. It may be that he is behind in preparing for a class in which you are completely up-to-date; in any event, it is helpful to establish mutually beneficial relationships with top students and to obtain top-quality fellow student outlines where possible. In addition, observe rules of common courtesy and proper etiquette. If a top student shares her outline with you on condition that you not circulate it to others, respect this stipulation, even if you would not place similar restraints on sharing your own work.

Hornbooks

Hornbooks are hardcover, scholarly treatises designed not as study aids, but as authoritative legal reference works. Lengthy and heavily footnoted, they are devoted to particular areas of the law and are written by noted legal experts, professors, and scholars. They are usually quite reliable, but since each hornbook consists of several hundred (or often over 1,000) pages of text, hornbooks are much too voluminous for busy law students to use regularly as study aids. You should therefore generally consult hornbooks infrequently, and then only to clear up any confusion that arises on particular or specific points of law. For example, if you did not understand the difference between a bilateral contract and a unilateral contract after a lecture and a review of other less detailed study aids, you could find the distinctive features of each amply discussed and illustrated in a hornbook on contracts.

Professional Publications, Inc. • Belmont, CA

By the same token, because of the detailed nature of hornbooks, a contracts hornbook would not be the best place to turn for a quick review of the subject, especially if you are only trying to gain an overview of the course and refresh your recollection for a final exam. Because of their bulk and hardcover format, hornbooks are expensive to buy, typically selling for $25 to $30 or more each. Happily, it is almost certain you will never need to buy one. The cost of using a hornbook can be reduced to nothing by making use of the hornbooks in the law school library. Given the small number of times you will find yourself needing to consult those treatises, there is little reason to purchase a hornbook, except perhaps for a class in which you are utterly confused or for which there are no other types of decent study aids available.

The following hornbooks are widely regarded as helpful to both students and lawyers:

- Calamari & Perrillo's *Hornbook on Contracts* (West, 2nd Ed., 1977)

- La Fave & Scott's *Handbook on Criminal Law* (West, 1972)

- Prosser & Keeton's *The Law of Torts* (West, 5th Ed., 1984)

West's Nutshell Series

Nutshells are akin to miniature, paperback hornbooks. West Publishing Company publishes dozens of nutshells on numerous legal topics, usually ranging from approximately 250 to 500 pages each. These study aids are less authoritative than most hornbooks (although a number of distinguished professors serve on the Nutshell Advisory Board) and vary greatly in quality. However, because they are fairly succinct as compared to hornbooks, nutshells provide a comprehensive view of the subject matter of a course with a minimum time investment on your part. The broad-brush treatment found in nutshells often serves to illustrate and focus one's attention on important legal issues that are likely to appear on a final exam, rather than on trivial minutiae. The nutshell series also covers considerably more course subjects than do outlines or hornbooks. Complete listings of the many nutshells and hornbooks published by West can be found at the beginning of any nutshell and should give you an idea as to what is available.

Canned Briefs

In our opinion, canned briefs are definitely something to avoid. These notoriously inaccurate study aids purport to summarize and brief the cases in your law school textbooks so that you will not have to. (As discussed in the chapter on studying, after a certain point it becomes a waste of time to fully and formally brief all such cases, but you should do so until you have mastered the art.) Your assigned cases, however, are already specially edited for law students and therefore are not more readily understandable in canned-brief form than when set forth in full.

Further, the holdings or central points of law of most of the cases you will read are stated accurately in reputable commercial outlines, all of which contain "Table of Cases" indices to help you locate the cases in the respective outlines. Thus, if you are using a commercial outline for a course, packages of canned briefs (even if accurate) will add nothing to your preparation except a loss of time and money.

Additionally, reliance on these "study aids" may lull you into a false sense of security, detract from your responses in class, and deprive you of practicing your own briefing and case-analysis skills. If you feel you absolutely must read summaries of cases, read those that appear at the front of each published opinion in most legal reporters found in your law school library. This is a cheaper and more accurate way of doing it than buying the packages of canned briefs in your local bookstore.

Black's Law Dictionary

During the first year of law school especially, you will encounter a multitude of unfamiliar terms in the course of your assigned reading. Words like demurrer, estoppel, waiver, deposition, mandamus, or jurisdiction may be crucial to your full understanding of a particular case or passage, even though they are not defined in your assigned reading. Since such terms (and many others like them) are integral parts of the language used by lawyers, it is imperative that you understand them in all their senses, and the sooner the better. *Black's Law Dictionary* is traditionally recognized as the leading dictionary of legal terms, and in our view it is a must for any serious student. First-year students should buy or borrow a copy of *Black's* to keep beside them at all times when reading assigned cases and materials. They should also immediately look up the definitions of legal terms they do not know. Though it may be somewhat expensive to purchase *Black's,* it is an investment in your legal career that will never stop paying off.

Professional Publications, Inc. • Belmont, CA

Law Professors

A law professor is a rich source of help and information that is typically underutilized by students. This may be because many law professors are perceived, whether accurately or not, as a little unapproachable. Even so, it behooves you to visit your professors at least a few times during the semester. After all, these professors will draft your final exams based in part on their own personal observations about the subjects they teach—observations that probably are not contained in any study aid or extracurricular source (except, perhaps, one written by them or a former student). Contrary to the popular myth, not all law professors are pompous old blowhards interested only in humiliating you. A great many are dedicated scholars and teachers who are genuinely interested in helping their students learn.

When you need help from a professor, do not put off visiting her until a few days before finals. If you do, you will find yourself in a tiny office surrounded by countless other half-crazed law students scrambling around trying to get a semester's worth of their questions asked and answered. (Many of these questions will, incidentally, be so bizarre and unrelated to the upcoming test that you will wonder whether you or the asker accidentally stumbled into the wrong office!)

This is not to say that visiting a professor a day or two before a final is never helpful, but by that stage there are probably more efficient uses of your time. As a general matter, it is also a good idea, psychologically speaking, to stay away from the law school entirely during finals, except to take the exams themselves. This will help you avoid the nervous tension and anxiety floating around all law schools during exam time.

Exam Files

Exams, like professors, evoke some unavoidable anxiety. One effective way of combating this anxiety while fruitfully preparing for the exam is through the use of another underutilized study aid—the exam file. In all law school libraries, you will find an exam file whose contents are organized by courses and professors. These files contain old law school exams, often written by your professors for the same courses you are taking. Such old exams will allow you to see the real thing—to glimpse, perhaps for the first time, how professors weave legal concepts into absolutely unbelievable factual settings (see App. E for some sample law school exams and answers).

By reviewing these exams prior to finals, you can avoid the nightmarish shock of trying to analyze in a few minutes the legal issues presented by a set of facts that probably took the professor days to dream up and that could not actually happen in a million years.

While exactly how and when to use old exams is discussed in the later chapter on studying, it is worthwhile to emphasize here that you should definitely make use of exam files as well as other study aids containing practice exams. What better way to get to know your professor's quirks and predilections than to familiarize yourself with tests he has deemed important enough to spring on earlier students? And although you should certainly not depend on it ever happening, professors have even been known to mistakenly reuse an exam already in the exam file.

Study Groups and Fellow Students

Study groups generally only work for first-year students. This is because first-years are assigned to particular sections where the same students are taking all of the same classes. Depending on whom you associate with at law school, there is a good chance that you will be asked to join a study group. Unfortunately, most law students do not have a clue as to what they are supposed to do in a study group. As a result, most study groups turn into gripe sessions about how difficult law school is and do not end up accomplishing much.

If organized properly, however, study groups can be beneficial. One of us participated in a very successful first-year study group. The group had four members and met once a week. Each member was responsible for outlining a week of law school classes for one particular subject for each meeting on a rotating basis. For example, for the first meeting of the group, student 1 was responsible for producing a written outline for a week of contracts lectures, student 2 was responsible for outlining a week of torts lectures, student 3 was responsible for outlining a week of property lectures, and student 4 was responsible for outlining a week of civil procedure lectures. The members of the study group were members of the same first-year section; thus they all had the same classes taught by the same professors. Each week the assignments were alternated, with each student being responsible for outlining a different class. The meetings for this study group were short, consisting merely of the students exchanging outlines and then discussing them. Each of the students in this study group finished at or near the top of his class.

Professional Publications, Inc. • Belmont, CA

There are several advantages to participating in a study group organized along the foregoing lines:

- It creates discipline and prevents procrastination and falling behind by forcing each of its members to outline her course material earlier in the quarter or semester than might otherwise be the case.

- The rotating assignments and equal workloads prevent one or more of the members of the group from being unduly taken advantage of, and allow each member to do outlining work on each of the classes he is taking.

- It allows group members to discuss course material and measure their progress against that of their fellow students without consuming an undue amount of time.

Thus, under the proper circumstances, study groups can be beneficial. To avoid problems, however, if you decide to form or join a study group, be sure to select people for the group who you like and who are not compulsive studiers. Teaming up with the wrong individuals will increase your anxiety and detract from, rather than enhance, your performance. If you do become involved with a study group that is not beneficial to you, is taking up too much of your time, or is otherwise counterproductive, do not hesitate to bow out gracefully.

Even if you do not participate in a formal study group, just talking about your course material with somebody in the course, even informally, can be very helpful to your understanding of the material. Simply verbalizing your thoughts will force you to clarify them in your own mind. Also, getting the benefit of someone else's perspective and understanding on a fairly frequent basis can help you judge your progress in a course.

Exam-Taking Aids

Law school bookstores are usually filled with publications that are supposed to help law students improve their test-taking skills. Such publications come in various forms from booklets on issue-spotting to flash cards. Some of these publications contain nothing but sample essay and multiple-choice questions and answers. Our feelings about these study aids is that they can help a student improve his test-taking skills. However, the benefit that can be obtained from using these study aids is generally of marginal value. Specifically, good practice exams can usually be found in sufficient quantities in the back of commercial outlines and in law school libraries. Generic test-taking publications mostly just duplicate, albeit on a larger scale, this material. In comparison to a review of past tests given by a student's professor, they also do little to prepare the student for the specific types of exams his professors are likely to give during finals. Thus, while there is some benefit to be obtained from test-taking study aids, using these aids is far from essential.

Wisdom Books and Other False Prophets of Truth

As a first-year law student, you will undoubtedly be inundated with unsolicited advertising for various forms of study aids, including lectures, tapes, and publications on how to take law school exams. This advertising is designed to exploit the fears of the first-year student. The advertising usually represents that whatever is being sold is essential for success in law school.

Such claims are generally falsehoods calculated to prey on the apprehensive student. As set forth in this chapter, while we believe that judiciously using certain study aids and avoiding others will allow you to maximize your performance, no particular study aid can "guarantee" your success. Success in any class, and in law school in general, depends in large part on hard work, savvy, and a knowledge of the big picture and the rules of the law school game. An ability to control the inevitable law school anxiety also helps a great deal. Once you fully understand how law school works and have thus removed ignorance, intimidation, and anxiety as roadblocks to your performance, success is largely a matter of hard work and individual ability. Not using a particular study aid, in and of itself, is not likely to prevent you from doing well.

Instead of latching on to a miracle study aid hyped by a false prophet as some kind of salvation for troubled law students, you must evaluate all study aids and guides with common sense. If certain advice does not seem right for you, even though it may work for others, do not follow it. There are few things about law school, aside from hard work, that are absolute musts. Many outstanding and equally successful law students have completely different approaches to outlining, briefing, and studying for exams. In these cases, hard work is the only common denominator and the equally excellent results obtained counsel against any hard and fast notion that there is only one right way. There is not, so do not be misled by false "prophets" in search of "profits" at your expense.

Professional Publications, Inc. ▪ Belmont, CA

Caveats: Warnings to Observe when Using Study Aids

Although the proper use of study aids can greatly enhance a student's performance, the improper use (or abuse) of study aids can have deleterious results. Therefore it is important to keep certain rules in mind when using study aids, and to observe the following caveats.

Do Not Go Overboard

Unfortunately, some law students suffer from the harmful delusion that if one commercial outline is helpful for a course, two such outlines must be twice as helpful, and even more so when used in conjunction with canned briefs, hornbooks, nutshells, bar outlines, and so on. Such academic overkill, however, is wasteful, time-consuming, expensive, and often confusing, such that any synergistic effect will most assuredly be negative. You honestly do not have to read every study aid ever produced on a subject to do well in your legal studies.

Generally, all worthwhile study aids on a given subject contain the same core information in varying amounts of detail (although inaccuracies, errors, and conflicts will inevitably be discovered). You are, for the sake of simplicity and a coherent approach to a subject, usually better off picking at most one commercial outline per course. A good commercial outline, if available, is generally the only written study aid (with the exception of *Black's Law Dictionary)* you will need to buy for a class. (As noted previously, bar outlines are unnecessary and probably undesirable; canned briefs should be avoided; hornbooks can be borrowed; law professors, exam files, and study groups are free; and fellow student outlines are not usually obtained by purchase.)

You may find it helpful to purchase an additional study aid, such as a nutshell, if you are having an especially difficult time understanding a particular area or concept of the law. Only in this limited situation, though, should you depart from the general rule of limiting yourself to one commercial study aid per course.

Study Only Relevant Sections

Law professors are continually amazed at the significant number of students each year who write on their final exams about topics that were never covered in class. This irrelevant discourse, no matter how internally consistent, does not impress law professors; rather, it annoys them and takes up valuable time that could have been used spotting and analyzing the real issues. Hence, it usually leads to disastrous exam grades. Therefore, unless your professor tells you otherwise, skip those parts of your study aids that cover topics not mentioned or discussed in class or addressed by one of your reading assignments. For example, if your criminal law professor has not covered the crimes of robbery and kidnapping in reading assignments or during her lectures, do not review those crimes independently hoping to show off your extracurricular knowledge on the final.

Most fair professors will cover final exam topics in both lectures and reading assignments, but do not be misled: any topic covered in either the assigned reading or the lectures is fair game for the final exam.

Because it is virtually guaranteed that topics boycotted by your professors will not appear on exams, if you miss a class, copy another student's notes or ask your professor what he or she talked about during the missed lecture. This will help ensure that you will not waste time reviewing irrelevant sections of study aids on the mistaken assumption that those topics were covered during class.

When Study Aids Will Not Work

Occasionally, you will find yourself in a class taught by an avant-garde professor who spends more time criticizing the law (or expounding as to what it should be) than teaching what it is. This professor usually adheres to an extremist view or approach that currently falls outside the mainstream of legal thought. Commercial study aids are not helpful for such classes since they reflect only accepted and mainstream legal thought.

You can usually identify avant-garde professors by their statements criticizing every U.S. Supreme Court opinion ever written on the topic they teach, or by their insistence that some arcane opinion written by a judge of a federal district court in Arizona constitutes the only correct statement of the law. In an amusing law school story related to the authors by a colleague, one of these professors had for days relentlessly criticized a line of Supreme Court cases, much to the irritation of the storyteller. After introducing a new case, the professor addressed this student with the question, "Mr. X, can you tell me what is wrong with the holding of this opinion?" Mr. X carefully replied, "I'm only a second-year law student. I wouldn't presume to tell five members of the United States Supreme Court that they have made a mistake." A deathly silence enveloped the classroom for a few moments, until the professor moved on to question another student; Mr. X was never called on again.

Discussing your professors with law students who have previously taken courses taught by them can also help you identify avant-garde types. When you determine that your professor is of an avant-garde mindset, avoid using commercial study aids unless you plan to drop the class for a more traditional one (not a bad idea in some cases). Instead, study solely from your class notes and any other material written, prepared, or assigned by your professor.

Think Independently

To be a good lawyer or law student you must not only understand what the law is on a given subject, but why it is. You need to understand the reasoning behind the law so that when a factual situation arises for the first time, you can venture an educated guess as to whether certain legal rules should or would apply.

Although study aids state what the law is, most study aids (hornbooks excepted) do not adequately explain the reasoning underlying the law. Consequently, even if you are intelligently using study aids to learn and organize the black letter law needed to pass your classes, you should still spend time reflecting on the reasoning underlying the law you are studying and whether (in your opinion) it makes any sense. Carefully read the cases for the rationales and policies underlying their holdings, and think independently about any common threads running throughout similarly decided cases. You need to do this so that you can reason by analogy on your exams, which will often require you to address issues that are not identical to any material previously studied. Many casebooks contain "Notes and Questions" sections following the edited opinions. Reading and struggling with these can promote independent thinking and provide new insights into the course material.

Subject to these caveats, using study aids judiciously is a big part of playing the law school game. At some point, one or more of your professors will probably warn you not to use any study aids whatsoever—an injunction probably stemming from an unreasonable fear that they will cause your legal reasoning abilities to atrophy. You should ignore any such warning, however well-intentioned—your professor is simply being overprotective. If you wisely use the previously discussed and recommended study aids, you will most likely find yourself better organized, informed, and prepared for finals than would otherwise be the case. Also, just as importantly, you will have more free time to enjoy your law school years.

Professional Publications, Inc. ▪ Belmont, CA

CHAPTER 7

Studying for and Taking Law School Exams

"Examinations are formidable even to the best prepared, for the greatest fool may ask more than the wisest man can answer."

— C. C. Colton, *Lacon*

A chapter on studying may strike you as superfluous. After all, you know how to study, or you would not be at law school, right? Well, yes and no. Law school subjects differ from most undergraduate courses, and the study habits you developed while pursuing an undergraduate degree may not translate well to the law school context. The purpose of this chapter is not to announce the only proper way to study in law school, but to suggest a general approach that has proven successful.

Generally speaking, your fellow law students will be brighter and more highly motivated than your undergraduate classmates were. You will be less able to coast during the year while relying upon natural ability and last-minute cramming to get good grades in law school. Also, most law school courses require the application of well-understood legal principles to a new fact pattern. They do not simply require a regurgitation of memorized facts, formulas, or concepts. Your studying needs to be consistent, sustained, and well-directed in order for you to succeed in law school.

This chapter will help identify successful study methods, and it will also discuss how other law students fit into your study program.

Gathering the Information

The two basic rules with respect to obtaining the information you will need to pass your courses are: read your assignments and go to class. This is pretty simple, but very important. Remember that law school classes impart to students an understanding of legal principles by examining a series of cases.

In class, the professor does not give a lecture that simply reiterates the information contained in the written opinions assigned as reading. Rather, the professor takes it for granted that the students have read the assignment and are in possession of the information it contained. Class time is spent in a question-and-answer session or in a discussion regarding the case. Through these activities, students are supposed to derive an understanding of the legal principles involved and to gain experience in applying legal principles to particular facts. Thus, if you have not read the assignment, you will miss much of the benefit of the in-class discussions because you will not understand what people are talking about. The importance of being prepared for class and not falling behind cannot be overemphasized.

Briefing

During the first part of your first year, at the very least, you should outline or *brief* the cases assigned as reading before the class session in which they will be discussed. Read all the way through an opinion, then go back and brief it. Your brief should include:

- the facts
- the holding
- the legal rules
- the reasoning

The *facts* generally are the operative facts of the underlying dispute or problem that gave rise to the lawsuit. In many cases, they will include the actions of the lower court or the procedural posture of the case. The *holding* means the action taken by the present court, distilled down to a single sentence. There can be more than one holding. The legal rules or *rationales* are the principles that cause the court to reach the decision it did. Legal rules are sometimes expressly stated by the court and sometimes must be derived or inferred. The part of the outline dealing with the court's *reasoning* is more amorphous. It can be a fuller explanation of how the legal rules resulted in the holding, or a statement of other factors the court seemed to find important. Of course, your brief must be concise enough that a quick review will permit you to respond intelligently to a question during class.

As previously mentioned, some publishers sell commercial case notes or canned briefs for the cases contained in the most popular casebooks. While these are tempting to use because of the perceived potential time savings, we strongly recommend that you brief your own cases and eschew canned briefs. Reading the case and briefing it yourself gives you a fuller understanding of the case. Additionally, your brief will reflect your understanding of the case and not that of someone else. Moreover, creating your own brief helps to crystallize the important aspects of the case in your mind.

Of course, briefing cases is time-consuming, and once you really get the hang of how law school classes operate, fully briefing all your cases in writing quickly reaches the point of diminishing returns. Briefing cases is valuable principally to focus your attention on aspects of the cases that are important from a legal standpoint, to make these points readily accessible for course outlining purposes, and to refresh your recollection of both the factual and legal aspects of the cases for purposes of classroom discussion. The process also helps you understand how case law is used as legal authority. You read cases in law school to learn legal rules and principles and why given factual situations give rise to particular results. You use the principles derived from this study to determine the probable results in slightly different factual situations, and to formulate arguments for one result or the other.

However, after a certain amount of practice reading and analyzing cases, you should not need to fully and formally brief each one. At some point you will be able to spot and retain the important points on your initial reading of the case. There are exceptions, though, where you should brief a case. For example, some second- and third-year courses are structured by the professor to maximize class participation by assigning cases to specific students for thorough analysis in class. When it is your turn, you will be expected to be able to expound on the assigned cases at length. Briefing the cases in this situation obviously will be helpful.

For the majority of second- and third-year courses, though, as well as first-year courses, once you understand what you are looking for in reading cases, full formal briefing is unnecessary. Careful reading before class and jotting down the case's key holding and rationale should suffice. *Book briefing* is a method of underlining or highlighting (sometimes with different colored markers according to a personal system) significant passages or sentences of the opinions in the casebooks. This allows students to quickly mark (and later quickly identify) the case's holding, legal rules, and other significant portions. After mastering the art of formally analyzing and briefing cases fully in writing, many students turn to book briefing as a way to save time and become more efficient.

Go to Class

Another important rule in obtaining the necessary information is "Go to class." As Woody Allen aptly observed, "Eighty percent of life is just showing up." It is true that class may be a frustrating experience from time to time. The Socratic method of teaching, still employed by many law school professors, often seems like a game of "hide the ball" or "guess what I'm thinking now." However, except in rare cases, the questions asked and the discussions initiated by the professor will provide some insight into the things she thinks are important and the way she thinks about the course material. If you only read the casebook and avoid going to class, you will lose the opportunity to gain these insights. These insights are extremely valuable, especially when exam time rolls around. Even if you have not prepared for class, you should attend.

Being prepared for class will also help you take coherent notes. Having good class notes is a fundamental requirement for doing well in most law school classes. For this reason, write your notes so that they are legible and easily understood. Short, simple sentences work best for this purpose. When taking notes in class, avoid the trap of trying to write down every word the professor utters; rather, you should focus on being sure to get all the main points of the discussion. Shortly after class, review your notes to make sure they are clear. If not, talk to your professor and fellow students to fill in any gaps. This little bit of extra work will yield significant dividends when you start outlining your courses.

If you cannot attend a particular session of a class, have a classmate tape-record the class. Supplying your own tape recorder and tape, as opposed to borrowing them, is preferable because you will impose less on your classmate, you will have more control over the quality of the recording, and you will have more flexibility in using the tape.

Listen to the tape recording of a class session you missed as soon as possible. Leaving all your tapes until the end of the term will overload you with unnecessary work at a critical time. Additionally, if you do not listen to the tape shortly after the class actually took place, your knowledge of the course will suffer from gaps. This can create difficulties in integrating the course material into an understandable framework. As you listen to the tape, take notes just as you would in class. While you may miss some of the conversation, you can control the speed with which you listen, starting, stopping, and replaying the important parts. Attending class sessions is preferable to listening to tape recordings, though, because you can participate in the discussion, ask questions, hear remarks from different areas of the room, and better understand and follow the discussion. However, listening to a good quality tape recording is a workable "next-best" alternative.

If you are unable to get someone to tape-record a class session for you, try to obtain a copy of someone else's notes from the session you missed. If possible, establish a reciprocal relationship with someone who takes good notes. You give him your notes for classes he missed, and he gives you notes for classes you missed. In this way, each person gains from the relationship.

As with the tapes, review the notes as soon as possible. The person who made them is more likely to be able to clarify them shortly after the actual class session than several weeks or months later. Additionally, delay will only make understanding the big picture of the course material more difficult.

Creating a Course Outline

For each class, we strongly recommend that you create your own course outline based primarily on your notes and briefs. While it is possible to wait until classes are over and to create your outline while studying for finals, it is much better to work on your outline periodically during the term, bringing it up to date every few weeks or so. That way you will not be overwhelmed by a massive amount of work at the end of the term.

Why Your Course Outline is Necessary

Creating your own outline organizes the course information and reinforces it in your mind. The course material is reinforced as you re-read your notes and briefs, as you think about how the material fits into the overall scheme of the subject matter, and as you physically write or type out the outline. Each step in outlining imprints the voluminous material on your mind again and increases the probability that you will remember it at exam time. Additionally, as you struggle to organize the course material into a coherent framework for your outline, you may come to understand it better. Just thinking about it again may lead to new insights or cause mental light bulbs to flash in a new way. Being able to review the material as part of a larger whole (in the context of what has gone before and what has come after) also enhances your understanding of it.

Creating an outline also helps to reduce the massive materials you will cover into a text of distilled legal principles of manageable length. You cannot possibly reread your 1,000 page (or more) contracts casebook while studying for finals; even if you could, you could not retain the large volume of information you had just read. Furthermore, even if you could memorize the entire book, much of the information would be useless and irrelevant detail that is of no help to you come test time. You can, however, read and reread a 40-page outline of your contracts course, containing all relevant rules and principles, many times just prior to taking your exam. Viewed in this way, the critical advantage offered by outlining is apparent.

If you are somewhat compulsive and have the time, you can outline week-by-week during the term. On balance, we do not recommend that you spend that much time in this endeavor. We do recommend that during the term you make a substantial effort every few weeks to outline the material already covered by your classes. This lessens the amount of outlining you will have to do later while getting you started when the early material is still fresh in your mind. Try to schedule your outlining intelligently by staggering it so you do not burn yourself out by having to outline all your classes at once.

The vast majority of the information that you will incorporate into your outline will come from your class notes and briefs. To fill in any gaps, you may need to read certain portions of the casebook over again or use a commercial outline.

Organizing Your Outline

The organization of the outline should reflect your personal understanding of the material covered. In most cases, the organization will flow naturally from the order in which the professor presented the material, although the degree to which this is true varies depending upon the professor. Your notes from classes taught by some especially fastidious types will already be very similar to outlines. Some professors practically outline the course for you on the blackboard every day. Classes taught by other types of professors will require greater effort to organize the material.

If you are confused about how to organize the course material in your outline, look at the table of contents in your casebook and/or a commercial outline. Use these as guides along with your notes and briefs. Remember that your outline should reflect your understanding of the material, not somebody else's understanding. If this approach still does not help, try to borrow another (successful) student's outline and copy it.

The size and detail of your outline will vary with the volume of course material and with individual preference as to the amount of detail necessary for effective reinforcement. Generally, handwritten outlines covering a one-semester, first-year class that met three hours per week seem to fall into the 25–45 page range. Except for constitutional law classes, where the legal principles involved are much more abstract and often involve a balancing of competing policies, extensive details of individual cases usually do not belong in the outline. You should be looking for the principles and rules that the cases stand for, not all the factual details of individual cases. Remember that your outline is your road map for the final exam, so make it as complete as it needs to be.

Having a computer to create your outlines is very helpful, if you can afford to purchase one. Some distributors sell software specifically designed to help law students organize their course material into outlines. Such software is not necessary, however. What is necessary is a good word-processing program like WordPerfect or Microsoft Word. A computer and such software will save you a lot of time and make organizing your outline easier.

Using Outside Sources and Study Aids Effectively

Generally, the vast majority (and many times all) of the material you will need to command in order to do well on the final exam is available from your casebook, briefs, and class notes. Many professors recommend outside reading, but usually they do so from the perspective of broadening your horizons, not assigning you additional material that must be briefed, memorized, and mastered.

In a code- or rule-related class, the set of statutes or rules involved also must be read and understood. Examples are the Federal Rules of Civil Procedure in a civil procedure class, or the Bankruptcy Code in a bankruptcy class. By "understanding" such materials, we mean that you should possess a working knowledge of the codes and rules and be familiar with their organization—not verbatim memorization. Do not attempt to use the code or rules as a framework for your outline, because they were probably not organized the way you need to organize your outline for class purposes. While the individual code provisions or rules may well become incorporated into your outline, you should fit them into the framework of the course material, not vice versa.

In some classes, an outside set of relevant rules may exist but not really be central to the course material. Examples are the Uniform Partnership Act in a business organizations class, or the Model Penal Code in a criminal law class. Such codes may or may not have been adopted, in whole or in part, as the law within the relevant jurisdiction. Even if such model codes or uniform acts have not been adopted in your state, your professor may still wish to use them as teaching tools, comparing and contrasting their provisions with the actual statutes. You will have to take cues from your professor as to how familiar you should be with such outside materials.

Hornbooks and commercial outlines should also be used as guideposts when you become conceptually lost. They should not be used as sources for learning vast amounts of course material, though, unless your professor is truly inept. In these rare situations, turn to the commercial course outline, learn the black letter law, and hope for the best on the exam. The commercial course outline will contain most of what you need, and the hornbook can be relied upon for more expansive treatment of an area you still find cloudy.

Generally, however, your resort to these outside sources should be purposeful and limited. The hornbook provides a scholarly exposition on basic legal principles germane to a given subject. Thus, hornbooks are most useful in shedding some light on areas in which classroom discussions or the assigned reading may have left you puzzled (such as, perhaps, when you are trying to figure out the role of foreseeability in the negligence cause of action, or the concept of proximate cause).

Carefully read the section dealing with the area causing your difficulty. Do not attempt to read the hornbook cover to cover or to use it as the primary source of information on the course. It contains far more information than you need at this stage—and far more than most people could digest and retain.

As mentioned before, commercial course outlines are useful in providing a starting point for your own outlines, and in studying or clarifying course concepts as well. In contrast to hornbooks, commercial outlines are written with the law student specifically in mind. They therefore tend to provide an appropriate (and not excessive) amount of detail on the subject matter. Hornbooks are designed for use by lawyers, judges, and legal scholars (not just law students). Thus, of necessity, they serve as bulky reference works and legal research tools. Since law students are generally interested in a brief, straightforward statement of the pertinent rules, commercial outlines (not hornbooks) are the more efficient source for getting the big picture.

Studying for Law School Exams

Most law school courses have only one exam at the end of the quarter, semester, or year, which may be a midterm or final exam, depending on the course length. Most exams are three hours long and contain three to five essay questions. The questions set forth a long, factual situation followed by something on the order of, "Discuss the rights and liabilities of the parties."

The fact that each course usually only has one exam obviously increases the importance of your performance. The basic steps in studying for law school exams are:

1. Finish and review your outline as discussed previously.
2. Take practice exams.
3. Create a mini-outline and flow charts.
4. Take care of yourself.

Taking Practice Exams

Once you have finished your outline, test it by taking practice exams. As discussed in the chapter on study aids, most professors put old exams on file in the law school library and some even provide model answers. Photocopy some of these and take them home. Read a sample test question and outline your answer without reference to your outline. Then compare your answer with the model answer, or if there is no model answer, use your course outline to review and evaluate your answer.

Taking practice exams, preferably under exam conditions, is the single best, and most often underutilized, method of preparing for exams. If you are a member of a study group, take practice exams with your group and evaluate each other's answers. Ideally, the members should find the same issues in the practice exam questions and reach the same depth of analysis.

If your professor does not keep old exams on file, check to see if another professor teaching the same course does. (Using your professor's old exams, however, is preferable because it gives you insights into how your professor thinks about the subject matter and how she likes to structure her exam questions.) If there are no old exam questions at all on file in the school library, use the sample essay questions in the back of commercial course outlines. These always have sample answers together with references to the text.

The vast majority of law school exams contain only essay questions. A minority of exams contain short answer (fill-in-the-blank) or multiple-choice questions. Another distinction among exams is whether they are open book or closed book. The majority of exams are closed book, which means that no materials may be referred to during the exam. Open-book exams vary in what materials may be used. Some code-oriented courses, such as Uniform Commercial Code courses, permit reference to the code only during the exam. Other exams permit students to refer to whatever written materials they want during the exam.

Use IRAC in Your Exam Answers

Answering law school exam essay questions is a specialized skill. Your objectives in answering essay questions are:

1. Identify the legal *issues.*
2. State the legal *rules* applicable to those issues.
3. Discuss the *application* of the rules to the facts presented in the questions.
4. State a *conclusion* as to the proper resolution of the issues.

(The common acronym for this method is IRAC, taken from the key italicized words from each step.) Identifying the legal issues is half the battle. Most of the time, the issues that appear on the final examination will be issues that were discussed in class, which is an important reason to attend class regularly.

The legal rules must be memorized. This is what is known as black letter law, and it is readily available to you from sources previously discussed. Creating a course outline from your class notes, briefs, commercial course outlines, and an occasional reference to hornbooks will give you a good grasp of the black letter law. You need to know the black letter law and be able to state it clearly and correctly in your answer in order to pass a final examination. Additionally, knowing the black letter law enables you to identify pertinent legal issues.

Discussing the application of the black letter law to the facts presented by the examination question is fairly straightforward and should flow naturally (but not mechanically) from the statement of the legal rule. For example, a torts examination answer discussing negligence issues arising in the context of an automobile accident might read in part as follows:

Plaintiff's Comparative Negligence
Regarding the Auto Accident

An important issue is whether plaintiff's own conduct will legally bar him from recovery in whole or in part. The doctrine of <u>comparative negligence</u> operates to reduce a Plaintiff's recovery in the proportion to the degree to which Plaintiff's own negligence contributes to his injuries. Additionally, in some jurisdictions if the negligence attributable to a Plaintiff contributed more than fifty percent to his own injuries, Plaintiff will be barred from recovering anything. Plaintiff's conduct will be held <u>negligent</u> if it fell below the <u>standard of reasonable care</u>—what a <u>reasonably prudent person</u> would have done in the same circumstances.

Here, Plaintiff was intoxicated and exceeding the posted speed limit by thirty-five miles per hour at the time his vehicle collided with Defendant's truck stalled on the highway. Plaintiff's conduct thus fell below the standard of reasonable care in two respects—in driving while intoxicated and in substantially exceeding the speed limit. Plaintiff's negligent conduct was a <u>but-for cause</u> of the accident because had he not been intoxicated and speeding, he probably could have reacted in time to avoid the accident. Plaintiff's conduct was also a <u>proximate</u>, or <u>legal</u>, <u>cause</u> of the accident, since it was very near in time and place to the accident, and it was <u>reasonably foreseeable</u> that speeding while intoxicated would hamper one's ability to safely negotiate unexpected obstacles, which frequently appear in the road, such as stalled vehicles. For these reasons, even if Defendant were also negligent to some degree in failing to anticipate the mechanical problem with his truck, Plaintiff's conduct was overwhelmingly responsible (more than fifty percent) for causing the accident. Therefore, Plaintiff probably would be barred from recovering anything for his injuries from Defendant, or in any event his recovery would be substantially reduced.

The conclusion usually is the least important part of an essay answer. While in some code- or rule-based courses, only one conclusion can properly be drawn under the rules, the majority of essay questions provide plenty of room to argue both sides of an issue. In fact, professors usually present "gray area" issues on exams that could go either way. They are looking for analysis and argument rather than a single correct answer. Therefore, your conclusion will be far less important than how you arrived at it.

While the IRAC method works fine for most law school essay exams, this is not always the case. In some classes, particularly those dealing with constitutional law, your professor may write an exam that raises issues that are not covered by any existing legal principles or black letter law. When faced with such a test, you should state the legal principles that come closest to addressing the issues on the exam. You also should discuss which (if any) of these principles should govern the matter at hand. You may, for example, want to reason by analogy that an established principle governs the hypothetical, or that public policy precludes its application. Further, your analysis should include a discussion of whether the rationale behind the rule or principle in question would be served if it is applied to the given facts. You could also consider proposing an entirely new principle of law to fit the specific facts on the exam. Such a principle should be based on logic, equity, public policy, and common sense.

No matter how you go about answering an exam question, use complete sentences. Avoid fragments or terse, mechanical expositions of the issues, rules, and applications. Remember that professors will be judging you against your classmates based on writing ability as well as substantive knowledge—both are very important. Note that the preceding sample answer makes good use of headings and underlining to organize and emphasize its points in a logical and clear manner. Your law professor will appreciate your use of such techniques provided they are not overdone.

Mini-Outlines

After getting a feel for answering essay questions by taking practice exams, you should go back over your entire course outline. The practice exams, by their nature, only cause you to review those areas of the course material raised therein. They are likely not inclusive of all matters that you must study to properly prepare for your final exams. You may find that creating mini-outlines or flow charts are helpful ways to review the entire course material. Your mini-outline should condense your course outline to five or six pages, using only bare-bones, memory-triggering phrases with no extraneous detail. The physical process of writing the mini-outline reinforces the material and also creates a more workable set of notes for repeated review.

Of necessity, the mini-outline will omit many details and will cover only the major points of a class. However, by this time, reading only a few words relating to a major point should trigger your recollection of a whole host of related rules on that point. This is one reason why the organization of your outline is so important. Placing unrelated things together in your outline will interfere with this triggering function. This is also why it is important to create your own outline. If the outline does not reflect your understanding of the course material, how you learned it, and how it fits together, it will not facilitate the necessary triggering. (A sample course outline, mini-outline, and flow chart are included in the appendices.)

Stay Healthy

It is important to maintain your physical and mental health while in law school. This means eating right, getting enough sleep, maintaining your hygiene, and getting enough exercise. Do not let exams disrupt your normal living routine too much. If you do not take care of yourself and as a result get sick during exams, your exam performance will suffer because you have to contend with your illness as well as with the exams.

Taking a break from studying to get some physical exercise not only keeps you physically healthy, but also refreshes your mind for the work ahead. Thus, you are more efficient in studying. You may also have an unexpected inspiration while jogging, bicycling, or working out. The benefits of exercise are well worth the hour or so it takes away from studying.

It is also worthwhile to take an occasional break and participate in some sort of social activity—just to act like a normal human being for a while. It lessens your anxiety to have contact with the outside world, and such contact puts law school exams into a broader perspective. Lessening your anxiety is important to your personal well-being because overwhelming anxiety tremendously impairs your ability to perform well on an exam. Anxiety can produce a mental gridlock, which obviously leads to poor results. (For additional tips on avoiding these problems, consult the chapter entitled "Maintaining a Life Outside of Law School.")

Taking Law School Exams

Finally, a few tips on actually taking the exams are in order. These tips are designed to maximize your performance, reduce your anxiety, and put you in as calm a frame of mind as possible.

First of all, make sure you have plenty of writing implements and paper or exam booklets. Also, before the day of the exam, confirm where and when it will be held. Give yourself plenty of time to get to the exam punctually, taking traffic, parking problems, and the like into account. Leave yourself at least 10–15 minutes to spare, but do not arrive hours before the exam and work yourself into a frenzy in the exam room before the test begins.

Once you get to the exam room, get settled and comfortable. If the exam is open book, arrive early, select a comfortable seat, and arrange your other materials for easy reference. If you are going to review anything at all, review your mini-outline or flow charts, with occasional reference to your course outline to refresh your recollection on specific points, if necessary. Do not attempt to learn new or additional material—it is far too late for that. Limit your discussions with other exam takers to subjects outside the exam course—sports, the weather, politics, anything but law. ("Do you think *res ipsa loquitur* will be on the exam?" "*Res* who?") Otherwise, you may find yourself anxious and confused at a most inopportune time.

Law school exams are taken anonymously. Each student is assigned an identifying number to be placed on the exam answer. Thus, the professor grading an exam answer does not know the student's identity. This procedure is designed to eliminate any personal bias from entering into the grading process. You therefore should put aside whatever hopes or fears you may have about your professor's feelings toward you and concentrate on producing objectively good answers on the exam.

Once the exam begins, budget your time carefully. Quickly flip through the exam to see how many questions there are and how much time you have to spend on each. Many times, the professor will give a time recommendation for each question. In answering each question, allot the first third of the time you have to reading the question and outlining your answer. This leaves you with the remaining two-thirds of your time for actually writing and revising the answer. Outlining is important because your answer should discuss issues in a logical sequence.

Do not let yourself run more than a few minutes over the allotted time for any one question. Having partial answers on all questions is better than some good answers and some blank ones. If you have time at the end, you can go back and finish an answer.

If you draw a blank on a question, skip it and answer another question first. There are no rules that state you have to answer the questions in sequence. After answering one question (and calming down a bit) you will be better able to think about and formulate an answer to the question on which you drew a blank earlier. If you still draw a blank, leave it to the end, and then just make something up as best you can.

You will probably have a choice of writing or typing your answers. Type your answers only if you have confidence in your typing, remembering that during the exam you will be nervous and under great time pressure. If you intend to type your answers, you should also ensure before exam time that your typewriter is functioning properly and has plenty of ribbon. If you write your answers, make your handwriting as legible as possible. You will receive no credit for a brilliant answer written in indecipherable hieroglyphics. Consider printing instead of writing in cursive, and double-space your lines.

If you diligently follow the principles of study, preparation, and exam-taking discussed in this chapter, we have no doubt that you will find your first, and subsequent, years of law school to be successful and rewarding.

CHAPTER 8

Choosing Second- and Third-Year Courses

"The strongest principle of growth lies in human choice."
— George Eliot, *Daniel Deronda,* Act VI, Scene XLII

Generally, your courses will be assigned for you in the first year of law school. However, you will have much greater flexibility in choosing your courses for the second and third years. Though there will be a few required courses and an overall number of credits needed for graduation, what you study in your second and third years will be largely up to you.

Core Courses

We strongly recommend that you take the traditional core courses that were not part of the first-year curriculum at your law school. Definitely included in this group are the subjects covered on the Multistate Bar Examination (MBE). The MBE is part of the bar exam for virtually every jurisdiction in the U.S. It is a six-hour, multiple-choice test covering six subjects: contracts, constitutional law, criminal law and criminal procedure, property, evidence, and torts.

Other core courses are corporations (or business associations), civil procedure, federal courts, remedies, probate (or wills and trusts), and professional responsibility (or ethics). Professional responsibility is part of every jurisdiction's bar exam, and a majority of states require taking the separate Multistate Professional Responsibility Examination (MPRE). The MPRE is a 50-question, multiple-choice test given three times a year, not coinciding with the main bar exam.

In creating your own list of core courses, you would be well-advised to determine the subjects covered on the bar exam of the state in which you desire to practice. If that state tests a subject not listed previously, consider it to be a core course for you. There is considerable variation from state to state of subjects covered on the bar exam.

Obviously, one reason for taking core courses is to increase the probability that you will pass the bar exam. It is possible to learn a subject well enough to pass the bar exam from a bar review course alone. However, it is much easier if you already have a working knowledge of the subject; then the bar review course functions as a true review.

Another reason for taking core courses is that well-educated lawyers are conversant with these areas of the law. In real life, these subject areas overlap and interrelate with each other. Possessing a general knowledge of these areas gives you, in the legal field, what E. D. Hirsch refers to in a more general sense as cultural literacy. *Cultural literacy* is a collectively shared body of knowledge, such that communication between members of that culture is enhanced and facilitated by the ability to immediately grasp a particular principle someone else refers to, and to properly understand allusions and analogies. For example, if a judge makes a witty allusion to the rule against perpetuities during oral argument and you merely stare dumbfounded at her, you may not lose the motion but you will have lost effectiveness and stature.

In addition to core courses, there are other courses that should be seriously considered for inclusion in your second- and third-year curricula. These include taxation, administrative law, the Uniform Commercial Code (UCC), and bankruptcy. The UCC in particular has some overlap with the contracts subject on the MBE. However, these subjects are also important for post-bar exam life because their rules and principles can have an impact on many other areas of law. For example, there are significant tax consequences to many decisions in "unrelated" areas of the law.

Beyond these recommendations, your choices should be guided by your personal preferences. You may decide to emphasize a particular area in which you think you might be interested in practicing, such as taxation, environmental law, public interest law, or international law. This emphasis can be a positive factor when you begin interviewing for legal jobs, and even if you ultimately decide to avoid that practice area, you will have added intellectual breadth to your study of the law.

Professional Publications, Inc. ▪ Belmont, CA

Clinical and Seminar Courses

In addition to traditional classes, most law schools offer clinical courses. These courses are designed to more closely approximate the actual practice of law than are traditional law school courses. Recall that the traditional law school class essentially entails attempting to derive black letter legal principles from case-analysis and question-and-answer sessions conducted by your professors. Clinical courses, on the other hand, give the students hands-on experience in discovery or trial practice. In these classes, you actually get to draft and answer interrogatories, conduct cross-examination of a witness, or engage in similar activities.

Clinical courses can be very valuable depending on the quality of the instructors. You should talk to other students who have taken a clinical course to evaluate the probable quality of the course before signing up for it. A good course can impart insights you might otherwise not gain in five years of practice. Alternatively, it might simply be a less intellectually challenging way of filling a spot on your course schedule.

There will also be a number of seminar-type courses offered. Compared with traditional law school courses, seminar courses tend to involve much smaller numbers of students, closer relations with the professor, more free-flowing discussion of the subject matter, and grading based on class participation and written papers as opposed to examination scores. The subject matter of seminar courses also tends to be specialized. If the seminar format appeals to you and you find the subject matter offered of interest, a seminar course may be a useful and rewarding addition to your course schedule.

Finally, some students select second- and third-year courses based on the particular professor teaching the course. Although rare, some professors are so bad they should be avoided, and you may want to delay taking a desired course in order to get a different professor. At the other end of the spectrum, a professor may be so wonderful that students sign up for his course even if they have no independent desire to study the subject matter. Generally, however, the professor should not be a predominating factor in choosing courses.

What to Look for in Your Courses

Second- and third-year courses differ from first-year courses. Your professors will assume that you have adapted to law school and therefore will expect more from you. The amount of material you will be expected to cover will be much greater because it will be assumed that you are a more efficient learner. At the same time, much of the anxiety associated with the first year will have dissipated. The pressure to get good grades will have usually lessened, and students will not feel the same need to demonstrate their interest in class.

Selecting courses you have an interest in helps combat the post-first-year problems of being overworked and bored. If you find the material interesting, it is easier to read and learn it, and it is (rather obviously) easier to remain interested and engaged during class.

Your overall course load should be balanced and workable. Do not overload your schedule, either on an overall basis or on a daily basis. Do not take too many difficult courses or courses requiring a great deal of work during the same semester or quarter. Pay attention to the dates of the final exams for each of your proposed classes to avoid conflicts or back-to-back exams. Most schools allow students to drop and add classes during the first week or so of class; this will permit you to make some last-minute adjustments to your schedule.

Finally, be aware that many courses have limited enrollments, so you should submit your requested course schedule as soon as possible after the law school office begins accepting them. This obviously increases your chances of getting the courses you want. Additionally, if a course you strongly desire to take is always overenrolled, request it at the first opportunity. If you wait until the last semester or quarter of your third year, you might miss the opportunity to take it.

During your second and third years, you largely control your courses. You should select courses to fulfill three goals. The first goal is to prepare for the bar exam. The second is to become well-educated in the major or traditional areas of the law. The third is to maintain your personal interest in law school. Keeping these goals in mind when selecting second- and third-year courses should increase both your success in and enjoyment of law school.

You should view having the freedom to choose your own courses as an opportunity to enhance the mental stimulation and academic challenge inherently offered by law school. Do not lose sight of the fact that the study of law, when approached with the right attitude, can be enjoyable and intellectually satisfying.

PART 3

Law School's Extracurricular Activities

Chapter 9: Maintaining a Life
            Outside of Law School

Chapter 10: Law Review, Law Journals,
             and Moot Court

Maintaining a Life Outside of Law School

"As plants are suffocated and drowned with too much moisture, and lamps with too much oil, so is the active part of the understanding with too much study."

— Montaigne, *Essays* LXXV

All law students need a life outside of law school, if for no other reason than to stay normal and sane. If you spend every conscious moment thinking about law school, not only will you go bananas, but you will likely become burned out and not do as well academically as you would otherwise. All work and no play is simply not a recipe for success or happiness.

During law school, you will undoubtedly meet students who spend all their time studying or talking about the law. They can be found most hours of the day or night holed away in their assigned study carrel, complete with bedding, alarm clock, and coffee machine. Their idea of a big night out is a trip to the law school vending machine. A casual observer might wonder whether these people have homes. They also never seem to be happy, since they are always worrying about some test or other hurdle they will face down the road. They erroneously consider their own mental well-being irrelevant. These students may be at or near the top of the class, but just as often they are only achieving average grades. As one quickly finds out, attempting to study 18 hours a day or more is counterproductive and quite silly.

Based on our collective experience, we truly believe that optimum law school performance can be obtained by combining rest, relaxation, and physical activity with hard work. Students need to keep their perspective balanced and develop or maintain a social life outside of law school. The easiest way to do this is simply to continue during law school to do those things that you enjoyed before. For example, if you liked going to the movies prior to law school, continue to go to movies once school starts. If you enjoyed working out at a health club prior to law school, continue to do so after you enter law school. In short, do not entirely stop doing the things you enjoy simply because you are enrolled in law school. While we do not suggest you try to emulate Axl Rose's social calendar, we do strongly recommend that students take the following steps to maintain a healthy, balanced social life during law school.

Go out socially at least one night every week. Whether it is dinner with family or spouse, a basketball game with friends, an intellectually stimulating play, or a night at the opera, just go out. The key is regularly doing some social activity that takes your mind off of law school completely. Do not feel guilty; you will start the next day mentally refreshed and ready for your studies.

Try to take a day off once every week or two. Going to the beach, keeping a journal, wine-tasting, fly-fishing, writing letters, golfing, shopping, exploring by car, painting, writing poetry—the list of engaging activities with which you can fill a day off from classes, briefing, outlining, and studying is long. If you are caught up in your studies and other law-related activities, by all means take a day off, temporarily forget the stress of law school, and lose yourself for a whole day in a different activity—the more fun and frivolous the better. It will do wonders for your mental outlook. You will probably feel comfortable taking more days off after you have been in law school for a while and have gotten the hang of it. Hopefully, this book will enable you to do so a lot sooner than you otherwise would.

Eat and sleep right. Try not to let law school paranoia lead you to alter your basic schedule. Be good to your body and yourself. Do not overeat, binge, or skip meals; just eat regular meals as you did before. Also, pay attention to what you eat. High-fat and empty-calorie meals will, over time, diminish your energy levels and your general sense of well-being. You should also make sure you get as much sleep as you need each night. A lack of sleep can make even the simplest tasks seem more complex. Trying to expand your available study time by eliminating sleep or regular meals is a shortcut doomed to failure. Not only is the extra time gained for studying inconsequential from the "big picture" perspective, but by depriving your body of basic needs you will be reducing your stamina, efficiency, and mental alertness. This could lead to illness or chronic fatigue, which will put you behind in your studies.

Do not socialize exclusively with fellow law students. Although it is easy to fall into a pattern of socializing only with those persons you see most—fellow law students—fight against getting into this rut. During law school, try to see family and non-law student friends as often as possible. This will ensure that your time off is relaxing and refreshing, and does not always turn into a forum for stressful and unnecessary study sessions and legal arguments.

Get regular exercise. Even if regular exercise was not part of your basic routine prior to law school, you should make it so during law school. Exercise, besides its many health benefits, will keep your mind sharp and alert. A recent study even indicated that regular exercise strengthens the brain by increasing the number of blood vessels nourishing the cerebrum. The study of law is more like an academic marathon than a sprint, and it requires much physical endurance and mental discipline; both of these qualities are promoted by regular exercise. Regular exercise not only increases your endurance and clears your mind for hard study, but can give you a temporary "natural high" (because of the release of endorphins, often spoken of by runners) and a continued sense of well-being. In short, exercise is a great stress reducer. A lack of exercise, on the other hand, makes you feel mentally sluggish as well as physically tired.

Every physical and mental edge you can gain is important in law school and, in our considered opinion, exercise is an extremely important part of the law school routine.

Have a sense of humor. If you do not do well on a test, or are caught unprepared in class, try to see the humor in the situation—like a black comedy. Law students tend to take law school and life far too seriously. A good sense of humor is a valuable asset that many successful individuals possess. In a *Forbes* magazine survey, business executives were asked to describe the characteristics of up-and-coming employees. The executives placed a sense of humor at the top of the list. A good sense of humor is essential for getting a student through the trials and tribulations of law school.

Professional Publications, Inc. ▪ Belmont, CA

Nourish your spiritual well-being. No matter what you do, some things in life will go badly for you. When this occurs, besides a sense of humor, it helps to have a belief system to fall back on. Prayer or meditation puts things in perspective and infuses some calmness into the otherwise hectic world of a law student.

Follow the preceding rules, and in all likelihood you will do better academically than if you spent all of your time studying the law. You will also enjoy law school a lot more than many of your fellow classmates who will suffocate themselves with excessive studying.

CHAPTER 10

Law Review, Law Journals, and Moot Court

"What I have crossed out I didn't like. What I haven't crossed out I am dissatisfied with."

— Cecil B. deMille

Law Review and Law Journals

What They Are About

Law school is a maker of myths and many of these myths center around the student-run institution of law review. You may have heard that only the top students make law review, or that once you make law review the rest of your career is an easy ride to fame, glory, and riches. You may have also heard law review is a living hell, a slave galley of neurotic and overworked law students being whipped by a crew of manic and frenzied editors into turning out reams of pedantic and verbose gibberish. You may have been told that law review is the only way to make it in the legal profession, or that it is the one aspect of law school to avoid at all costs in order to maintain your sanity.

Before discussing law review (or *law journal,* as it is called at some schools) further, we will try to debunk some of the myths surrounding it and state generally what it is and is not. Most good law schools, and all law schools that are truly well thought of, have law reviews.

Law review is an institution composed of and run completely by students, perhaps with some guidance from the faculty and financial support from the administration. It is dedicated to publishing scholarly articles on the law by law students, law professors, and other members of the legal profession. It usually publishes softcover volumes several times a year; each year these are bound into a large hardcover volume, sequentially numbered, and placed into a set of volumes previously produced by the particular school's law review. The number of schools producing law reviews and the volume of periodicals produced by these schools are so great that an entire floor of a good-sized law school library can be taken up by law review periodicals alone. Some schools' law reviews (such as Harvard's) date from the 1800s; others are of more recent vintage.

The quality of a school's law review reflects upon and affects the legal community's perception of the affiliated law school. If a law school's law review is a professional-quality publication presenting educational and interesting articles by eminent legal authorities, it reflects well on the law school itself and tends to improve the law school's reputation. Conversely, if a law review publishes thin, typo-laden, and sparsely footnoted texts comprised of work by inferior authors from little-known schools, the affiliated law school's reputation will suffer accordingly. If the members of law review, supposedly the cream of the student crop, cannot produce a good periodical, how good can the rest of the students and the faculty teaching them be? While this may be an oversimplification of the way in which a law school's law review affects its overall prestige, the axiom largely holds true.

In short, the quality of a school's law review and the perceived quality of the law school as a whole are interrelated. Authors mail manuscripts to many law reviews and, if multiple offers are received, they generally choose to publish in the law review from the most prestigious law school. Also, publishing an influential law review article that is cited by courts and legal commentators enhances the law review's reputation. A good law review benefits all students, and a bad law review (or no law review at all) works to their detriment.

Aside from enhancing the school's reputation, what can a law review do for students? Since we are now speaking of individuals rather than law schools, the answer is that it can do nothing for them unless they participate.

There are pros and cons to law review participation. On the upside, law review participants hone their legal citation and research skills and often acquire immensely helpful writing and editing skills. They gain exposure to areas of law not taught in the law school curriculum and attain the prestige and distinction of being part of what most people consider to be their school's best legal journal.

On the downside, the law review participant must endure seemingly endless hours of burdensome cite-checking and rewriting article drafts, the loss of study time that could otherwise be used to improve the student's grade point average, and the loss of free time. Additionally, the participant may experience feelings of exhaustion, overwork, frustration, and even anger at law student superiors who, with complete license, ridicule, rewrite, and critique the participant's treasured work product. Further, only a very few law students—or, for that matter, law review participants—ever make it to the coveted status of editor, that jewel that lights up a law student's résumé like a Christmas tree ornament.

Our personal feeling is that the writing experience gained by anyone who sticks with law review is worth the long hours and unpleasant menial tasks encountered along the way. Reasonable minds could differ, however, and for that reason it is desirable, if you have any doubts, to gather all the information you can about your school's law review before deciding to join.

How Law Review and Law Journals Work

How one joins or becomes a member of a law review varies from one law school to another. At some schools, participants must be invited to join. Typically, these schools' law reviews require invitees to have demonstrated exceptional academic prowess; that is, they must fall into the top 10, 15, or 20 percent of their first-year class based on grades. Other schools are more liberal and allow candidates to "write on." This more egalitarian method is based on the philosophy that grades alone, for various reasons, are not the end all in assessing legal and writing skills. Students in these schools are invited to submit drafts and go to work for the law review cite-checking manuscripts, conducting office hours, answering the phones, and performing various other tasks. The law school usually awards minimal credit (such as one unit per semester) for the work of the invitees. Some schools' law reviews use a combination of the preceding methods of joining, inviting top grade-getters with formal written invitations while still allowing other students to write on.

The invitee will work hard. It is not easy to publish a thick, bound volume of closely reviewed and edited, and sometimes highly technical, scholarly articles each year. Each article contains up to hundreds of legal citations, mostly in footnotes, to the sources and supporting materials for the facts and propositions stated in the article. The footnotes, in turn, may contain string citations of case, statutory, and secondary authorities. The basic purposes of legal citation are to identify the source being cited, distinguish it from other sources, and help the reader locate the source (whether it be a case, statute, ordinance, treaty, treatise, book, article, or whatever).

Invitees are given sections of an article (for example, a portion of the text containing 20 to 30 footnotes) at a time to check. *Cite-checking* is the process of actually looking up the sources cited by the author and ascertaining whether they are in the correct form and support the stated propositions. After finding the source, the invitee must read it and make a critical judgment about whether it supports or does not support the author's proposition.

In addition, the invitees must carefully check citations for accuracy and style conformity with the elaborate rules and conventions contained in the Harvard Blue Book. *Blue booking* is a highly technical process that has in recent years been criticized by some notable legal scholars, including U.S. Court of Appeals Judge Richard Posner, for its fetish-like overattention to trivial detail. Like it or not, however, it appears that the numerous and technical rules of the Harvard Blue Book are here to stay and will probably plague law review participants for decades to come.

While the process of cite-checking is very time consuming, it familiarizes the cite-checker with various source materials, including landmark decisions and articles in the field. In addition, the process requires the exercise of critical judgment about whether a legal authority supports a given proposition. Exercising such judgment is something you will do over and over again in the course of your legal career, albeit in very different situations. However, whether you are reviewing a colleague's brief or analyzing an opponent's motion, exercising that critical judgment is the very essence of legal analysis. Participating in law review develops that skill.

Once the invitee meets all requirements for office and cite-checking hours and works during his free time to produce his own draft law review article of sufficient quality, he may be granted law review membership. Producing the requisite article usually takes several drafts, each of which is edited and critiqued by student law review editors who have gone through the process themselves already. These editors will help the student with writing style, citation form, and, to a lesser extent, the substantive aspects of his article. Depending on your editor's personality (or lack thereof), the experience can be a pleasant one filled with learning and helpful instruction, or it can seem like a frustrating encounter with an intellectual bully.

Slowly, with each redraft and through the editing process, the student's manuscript will change into a heavily footnoted, highly structured article. (Student articles, by the way, are not called "articles" in law review parlance; they are termed *notes* if they address only a particular case as their topic, and are termed *comments* if they have a broader subject. The term *article* is reserved for works by professors and other lawyers. The final published volume of a law review will include some student notes and comments, but will be comprised primarily of professional articles. For simplicity, however, we will use the common referent "article" unless otherwise specified.)

After still more drafts, each followed by more editing and criticism (as well as more work as a staff member), the student's draft may reach a stage where it is of a very high and nearly publishable quality. At this stage, it will have easily gone through over half a dozen drafts, and perhaps over a dozen. Based on the judgment of the editors reviewing the work (usually the editor-in-chief, the student notes and comments editor, and the particular editor assigned to edit the student's work), the student may then be invited to serve as an editor.

The complete transition from invitee to member to editor may take as little as one semester in the case of exceptional students, or as much as one and one-half years for others. Much will depend on the time and energy the student has to devote to her law review activities. Law school is certainly a demanding enough place without these additional law review burdens, and students participating should not be disappointed if they do not progress as rapidly as their law review peers.

For various reasons, the attrition rate of law review staffs is great. Many invitees and write-ons are weeded out by the onerous work requirements early on and abandon their articles in the early stages. Many feel they can expend only the time and effort it takes to obtain member status and thereafter abandon further work and writing, content with that level of accomplishment. Many, quite simply, cannot or choose not to keep up with the additional work augmenting the day-to-day grind of law school; they do not enjoy law review and value their free time too much to spend it that way. Very few attain the rank of editor by the end of the process; even fewer have their articles published in a law review, whether that of their own law school or another. To do either or both is evidence of diligence, perseverance, and the ability to work hard under trying conditions; it is no wonder that many law firms look favorably upon law school graduates who have been editors or have written published articles.

Law review is run by editors. The editor-in-chief is the most powerful and prestigious editor position. Other common editor positions that are well thought of are the managing editor, the articles editor, and the student notes and comments editor. The managing editor takes care of contracts and financial aspects of law review, including its arrangement with its publisher. The articles editor communicates with professionals whose articles have been accepted for publication and assigns the editing of their work. The student notes and comments editor performs the same function with student-written works.

Other editor posts include the research editor (who assigns cite-checking tasks to student members and invitees) and the executive editor. There may be many other editors with no specific responsibilities except to edit articles, a task common to all editors. The top editor positions are usually elected, with outgoing editors in the graduating class voting along with new editors, and perhaps members, who may be given half a vote. Other editor positions may simply be appointed by the editor-in-chief once the latter has been elected. The exact mechanics will differ, of course, from review to review.

There is no denying that there are politics involved in the functioning of law review. Decisions regarding whether to publish student articles or the articles of professors from the law review's own school, for example, are always touchy. Decisions on who will make editor, made by the cabals of editors discussed previously, are similarly sensitive. Law review editors are aware that they must preserve and enhance the quality of their product and that admission to their ranks cannot be made easy; they also realize that they, because of their editing and guidance role, play a large part in the success or failure of member and editor candidates. Further, they realize that they can be blamed for bad or controversial decisions. At the same time, the editors have a large book to put out and are thus motivated to help others attain editor status so that they can help with the burdensome task.

As in all working situations, some editors, members, or other law review participants may not always get along. It is, however, crucial to the quality of the final product, the success of the law review program, and ultimately the reputation of the law school that they work together as smoothly and efficiently as possible toward putting out their publication.

Alternative Journals

Membership in a law journal other than the main law review or journal published by your law school can also provide you with valuable writing and editing experience. The structure of the editorial hierarchy and the work involved in turning out a published legal periodical is generally the same in other journals as in law review. There are advantages and disadvantages to obtaining that experience with an alternative journal instead of as a member of law review.

Membership in an alternative journal does not carry with it the prestige of law review membership. It carries less weight with prospective employers and usually has less résumé value. Because the competition for membership in alternative journals is lesser or nonexistent, it represents less of an achievement than law review membership. Additionally, if you move into an editorial position, the minions doing your bidding will be fewer in number and generally less driven and dedicated. Thus, advancing into editorial positions in an alternative journal will not necessarily relieve you of lower-level tasks.

On the other hand, the fact that competition for membership is slight to nonexistent also makes for a more relaxed, less stressful atmosphere. The members of an alternative journal are voluntarily bound together by a common interest in the specialized subject matter of that journal instead of being driven together by their need to achieve something. In comparison to traditional law reviews, there is substantially less competition for editor positions, which are often filled by those willing to dedicate the time necessary to keep the alternative journal alive. These factors tend to minimize the backbiting, politicking, and one-upmanship that can sometimes make law review unpleasant.

In addition, because the subject matter of an alternative journal is usually specialized, you have the opportunity to meet and work with outstanding scholars and practitioners in that area. Moreover, because the articles address an area of the law you already have an interest in, you can gain valuable substantive knowledge while preparing an article for publication. As with law review, though, the preparation of alternative journal articles for publication necessarily includes the drudgery of cite-checking.

A further advantage of membership in an alternative journal is that you are more likely to have your own comment or note published (if you are willing to make the substantial commitment of time and energy necessary to research, write, rewrite, revise, proofread, argue with student editors, and finalize such a work). There is simply less competition for the space in the journal. In fact, some alternative journals are chronically short of material to publish.

In sum, the experience that can be gained from joining an alternative journal is valuable and potentially rewarding, but, like law review, it demands a substantial commitment of time and energy. Membership in a journal specializing in an area of law that holds particular interest for you can be especially worthwhile, not only in developing your legal writing skills and your knowledge of a substantive area of law, but also in making contacts with leading practitioners and scholars in the field.

Is Law Review for You?

Having read about law review and other journals, it will be up to the potential participant to gather more information and to make his or her own decision about whether to participate. If approached with the right attitude, law review can be a positive and enlightening experience not only in the areas of substantive law, but also in the sense of working with others toward a worthy goal. Good law review articles are often cited as persuasive by courts and may actually help shape the course of the law.

Although time consuming, law review is also rewarding. It is not a coincidence that many of those devoting much time to law review are simultaneously achieving the highest grades in their classes. The writing skills gained in editing your own work (and the work of law professors, if you become an editor) will aid you in countless ways throughout your legal career. Furthermore, having an article published and distributed throughout law schools nationwide produces a justifiable sense of accomplishment. For goal-oriented people who can see the light at the end of a long tunnel of hard work, law review can be a rewarding and invigorating challenge augmenting that posed by the law school curriculum.

However, it must be emphasized that law review is not for everyone. Many are simply not interested, dislike the regimentation and menial cite-checking aspects, and feel that their time would be better spent devoted to their other legal or personal interests. There is nothing wrong with the decision not to participate in law review and there are plenty of outstanding practitioners who never did. If law review is not for you, do not feel compelled to participate just because someone expects it of you, you feel you must, or because your father, mother, or great uncle did. It is an individual decision and only those who make it according to their own wishes will be able to derive from the law review experience all that it has to offer.

Moot Court

Moot court is generally an extracurricular activity in law school (although some law schools have a mandatory version of this activity as part of the first-year curricula). A legal question or issue is said to be *moot* when it presents no actual controversy, or where the issue has ceased to exist. Thus, moot court is a forum for law students to argue moot or hypothetical cases.

Participating in moot court requires researching and writing a brief, and then presenting oral argument before "judges" who will render a decision. Moot court is structured as a competition, which means that you will be arguing against other students and that one side "wins" and the other "loses." In some cases, there are additional levels of competition, up to the national level.

Moot court is valuable in the sense that the participants are doing things that real lawyers do; this aspect distinguishes it from most law school activities. Moot court presents law students with an opportunity to engage in the functional equivalent of handling a case on appeal following a trial court's judgment. Additionally, it provides students with experience in legal research, legal writing, and oral argument, which are all applicable to the more general practice of law.

Participants are paired and given certain basic materials, including the factual record and the decision that is the subject of the appeal. This is somewhat artificial in that a lawyer handling an appellate matter is required to have command of much more extensive materials, including all the papers and pleadings filed in the court below, transcripts of hearings, trial transcripts, trial exhibits, and jury instructions. It is necessary to use an abbreviated record to keep moot court manageable for law students.

Participants usually get to choose what side they want to represent, subject to the limitation that the exercise requires an equal number of *appellants* (the party appealing from the decision below) and *appellees* or *respondents* (the party that won in the lower court). Cynics maintain that selecting the politically correct party to represent increases your chances of doing well in moot court, which ultimately involves the exercise of subjective judgments. We would like to think otherwise.

Once you and your partner have settled on a side to represent, you will need to divide the issues on appeal for researching, writing, and arguing. The issues are normally well-defined by the materials you are given. If you are representing the appellee, this process is different from a real appeal because you are not responding to a particular appellant's opening brief; instead you are briefing the issues in a vacuum.

Legal research is a skill you will learn, use, and refine throughout your legal career. Researching your moot court brief provides you with an opportunity to practice that skill. If it seems like drudgery, be content with the knowledge that (unless you are one of those individuals who simply love it) legal research is and always will be drudgery to some extent.

There is no one right way to conduct legal research. The materials you are given will get you started. Hopefully, the issues involved will necessitate dealing with a limited number of important cases. The *Shepard's* citations system will give you other cases that have cited your initial cases for the same point of law. Those cases will lead you to other cases. Unless the issue is fairly abstruse, you can spend an infinite amount of time going from case to case by "shepardizing." Stop when you reach the point of diminishing returns or when you start coming back to the same cases.

Treatises, digests, statutory annotations, and the computer research networks LEXIS and WestLaw can broaden your research and give you additional starting points. Fortunately, today virtually every first-year law student learns how to use the computer research networks. Both LEXIS and WestLaw have data bases of almost every published case and permit users to conduct key word searches to hopefully find pertinent cases quickly.

The format used for writing the briefs is drawn from the *Handbook of Appellate Advocacy* or a similar text. The organization of appellate briefs follows a commonly accepted structure, and it should be adhered to even if certain sections seem redundant or unnecessary. Style is important. Some appellate courts strike briefs that do not conform to the required format. (When a court *strikes* something, it means that it is of no legal effect and is not to be considered.)

Citation format should be based upon *A Uniform System of Citation* or the Harvard *Blue Book* (discussed previously in connection with law review). This may seem overly formalistic, and perhaps it is. However, when you are attempting to persuade an appellate court by referring to a particular case, the court must be able to find the case before it can read it to see whether it supports your argument. It hurts your chances of winning if the court cannot readily find the case to which you are referring because you eschew conventional citation form.

Aside from adhering to proper appellate brief organization and proper citation format, the essence of legal writing is the art of persuasion. You bring the reader to the desired conclusion by logic, analogy, rhetoric, emotional appeal, and policy considerations. Your sentences should be short, clear, and in the active tense. Budget your time so that you can blend your polished sections with those written by your partner, and then revise and finalize the completed brief. You will not have an acceptable product if you attempt to knock out the first and final draft the night before it is due.

After the briefs are turned in, you and your partner are matched to an opposing team. You will be provided with your opponents' brief and an opportunity to research their cases and to prepare for oral argument. The *Handbook of Appellate Advocacy* deals extensively with preparing for and conducting oral argument, and this chapter is not designed as a substitute. However, a few good points are worth stressing.

1. Know the facts cold. You have the advantage of an abbreviated record, so gain complete command of the factual background.

2. Master the legal principles involved and the major cases cited in your brief and in your opponents' brief.

3. Prepare an outline for your argument. Do not simply repeat your brief and do not attempt to read from a verbatim written script. Your outline needs to be flexible enough to permit you to return to the thread of your argument after being interrupted to answer a question from the "court."

4. Practice your argument. That is not to say you should memorize it, but become comfortable with it. This is a great excuse for those who habitually walk around talking to themselves—now, you are just practicing oral argument.

5. Work with your partner to practice fielding hostile questions. You have to be able to deal with the points raised in your opponents' brief, and to persuade the "judge" that your position should prevail. Further, questions should be answered and not evaded. Nothing is more likely to annoy a judge than evading her questions.

6. At oral argument itself, conduct yourself as an officer of the court. Your dress and behavior should be appropriate and in keeping with the decorum of the court. You should always treat your opponents and the judges with professional courtesy. Anything less will detract from your stature as an advocate and from the effectiveness of your argument.

Whether to participate in moot court is an individual decision. It is extracurricular and takes a lot of time. However, it is generally scheduled so as to not interfere with preparations for final examinations. It is good experience and gives you as a law student a feel for real lawyering.

The résumé value of moot court is debatable. It will not compensate for poor grades and is not equal in value to law review. Conversely, if you have good grades, the absence of moot court experience will not hurt you. However, it is a positive factor, especially if you progress to higher levels. If your grades are fair to mediocre, having moot court on your résumé might be helpful in tipping the balance between getting and not getting a job offer.

PART 4

Law-Related Employment

Chapter 11: Job-Hunting Tips
for the Law Student

Chapter 12: How to Find Legal Employment

Chapter 13: Judicial Clerkships

Job-Hunting Tips for the Law Student

"Blessed is he who has found his work;
let him ask no other blessedness."

— Thomas Carlyle,
Past and Present Act III, Scene xi

Present Status of the Legal Job Market

Today's legal job market is far different from that which existed just a few years ago. In the 1980s, high-paying legal jobs were plentiful. Students graduating from a good law school with decent grades usually had several job offers to choose from. Second-year students were also swamped by offers of summer law firm clerkships, often sweetened by outlandish perks and a summer schedule packed with fun-filled, firm-sponsored activities. During the 1980s, salaries for lawyers continued to escalate dramatically each year as legal employers strove to keep pace with the seemingly ever-increasing demand for their services.

The boom time of the 1980s legal market is now gone, probably forever. Besides a general downturn in the economy, the rising cost of legal services has caused many businesses and individuals to try to avoid hiring lawyers whenever possible. Many corporations are restricting the amount of work assigned to outside lawyers by having more of their legal work done by in-house staffs. Large corporations have also started closely monitoring their monthly legal bills in an attempt to prevent their outside attorneys from undertaking and charging for all but the most essential legal tasks. The sharp and continual increase in the number of practicing attorneys has resulted in fierce competition for legal clients and less work for the average attorney. At the same time, constantly shrinking budgets have significantly cut the ability of numerous city, state, and federal agencies to prosecute or defend against legal actions. Not surprisingly, the demand for law students and recent law school graduates is noticeably lower than in the past.

Because of these new economic realities, law students now need to plan more carefully their job searches during and after law school. The days when an average law student could simply walk into her placement office, sign up for and attend a couple of interviews, and walk away with a good job are over. This chapter therefore focuses on ways you can increase the odds of finding legal employment in today's tough job market. It begins by setting forth general job-hunting tips for finding legal work throughout law school and upon graduation. Subsequently, specific guidelines and considerations pertinent to looking for work after your first, second, and third years of law school are discussed in detail. Working part time during law school is also discussed in this chapter.

General Job-Hunting Tips

No matter what type of legal job you are looking for, or when, the following general tips and guidelines should be kept in mind.

Your Placement Office and the NALP Forms

No matter what type of legal job you are looking for, your law school placement office is usually the best place to start. Therefore, you should visit your school's placement office immediately upon starting law school, or soon thereafter. Familiarize yourself with its resources. You should also introduce yourself to the director of the placement office (or his assistant) by making an appointment with him to discuss your long- and short-term employment goals and ways to attain them.

Most placement offices run on-campus interview programs for students seeking summer and post-graduate legal jobs. There are usually strict deadlines for signing up to participate in these programs. Traditionally, most law students have found work by participating in such on-campus interviews. Accordingly, you should find out when the sign-up deadlines are for your school's on-campus interviews, and comply with them well in advance.

On-campus interviews are usually held for second-year students seeking summer associate positions and third-year students seeking jobs after graduation. Employers schedule interviews during the first few months of the fall semester. Additionally, in the past, another set of on-campus interviews typically have been held during the spring semester for first-year students seeking summer jobs and for third-year students who have not yet found post-graduation employment. Although such spring interviews still exist, they are diminishing in number due to the economic factors discussed at the beginning of this chapter.

Virtually all legal employers participating in on-campus interviews will fill out and send to your placement office a data form published by the National Association for Law Placement (NALP). NALP is a nonprofit educational organization whose membership is drawn from both legal employers and law schools. It has generally been successful in setting uniform standards for interviewing and hiring law students. NALP Forms contain certain information about the legal employer in question, including the number of attorneys it employs, its primary areas of practice (for example, environmental, real estate, administrative, labor law, etc.), the number of minority or handicapped attorneys it employs, and the average number of billable hours its attorneys work.

The NALP Form also contains a section for the employer to list the person or persons responsible for administering or overseeing the hiring of attorneys and law students. Although this person's precise title varies from employer to employer, it usually is something similar to director of recruitment or hiring coordinator. The NALP Form also provides a space for a narrative statement concerning a legal employer's special characteristics, such as its work atmosphere. You should carefully read the NALP Forms for legal employers you are considering applying to for a job.

In addition to those legal employers who will be conducting on-campus interviews, there are some legal employers not interviewing on campus who are still interested in hiring law students from that particular school. Usually these employers also submit completed NALP Forms to that school's placement office along with letters expressing their interest in receiving résumés from the school's students. Such potential employers should be included in your job search.

Most placement offices will have a copy of NALP's *Directory of Legal Employers*. This directory contains NALP Forms for over 1,000 legal employers who are indexed by, among other things, geographical location, office size, and type of employer (Government, Corporate, Public Interest Groups, and All Employers).

WestLaw, a computer research data base, also contains NALP Forms. Most law students learn how to use WestLaw during their first year of law school and can access the system through computers kept in their school's law library. (Additional information on using WestLaw can be obtained by calling 1-800-WestLaw.)

You should use the NALP *Directory* to identify legal employers that seem suited to your abilities and interests, even if they are not interviewing on your campus. Before taking the time to send a résumé, however, call the contact person listed on the NALP Form to verify that the legal employer has some interest in receiving it.

The NALP *Directory* also contains the NALP Principles and Standards for Law Placement and Recruitment Activities (the NALP Guidelines). The NALP Guidelines set forth certain employment and job-seeking principles along with general standards for the timing and acceptance of offers. Almost all reputable legal employers and law schools abide by the NALP Guidelines. Employers generally expect that law students will abide by them as well. Accordingly, you should read the NALP Guidelines before you start your job search. Most placement offices provide copies of these guidelines to their students.

Besides NALP Forms, you also can find in most placement offices sign-up sheets for, or information on, various programs designed to help students increase their job-hunting skills. These programs often include mock interviews and résumé-writing workshops. You should take advantage of these programs if they are available at your school.

Your placement office should also have information on which legal employers have traditionally hired students from your school. Obviously, such employers deserve a closer look than those who have never hired a student from your school. Placement offices and your school's clerkship committee (if it has one) may be able to help students find judicial clerkships and externships; such positions tend to enhance a student's résumé and increase her marketability as a lawyer. Ads for part-time legal jobs are also normally listed or posted in the placement office throughout the school year.

In summary, familiarize yourself with and use the many resources available in your law school's placement office. Doing so will vastly enhance your job-hunting prospects.

Be Realistic

Your class standing and law-related accomplishments will have a major impact on your desirability to potential employers. In searching for a legal job, keep this fact in mind. While the number one law student at Harvard is going to have his pick of legal jobs, a law student at the bottom of his class from an unaccredited law school will not. There is a sliding scale of employability between these two extremes, which is where the vast majority of law students will find themselves. Accordingly, before you begin your search for a legal job, you need to honestly assess your perceived desirability as a legal employee. Generally speaking, legal employers consider the following factors in hiring law students:

- the quality of the student's grades and written work
- the rank or reputation of the student's school
- the impressiveness of the student's extracurricular activities (for example, did the student participate in law review, moot court, etc.)
- the student's prior work history

Further, there is an increasing trend by many legal employers to favor hiring minority and/or women applicants over other similarly qualified candidates.

If one or more of the foregoing factors mitigate against you, you should be less selective in deciding what legal employers to interview with during your job search. For example, some legal employers spell out on their NALP Forms that they only hire students in the top 10 percent of their class. Do not waste your time attempting to interview with such potential employers if you are not in the top 10 percent of your class.

Conversely, avoid interviewing with legal employers you are unlikely to accept a job offer from. As much as possible, try to target legal employers from whom you would probably accept an offer. If, for example, you have a family in California and you want to stay in the state, do not send your résumé to a New York law firm. Similarly, if you like having some free time, do not bother interviewing with a big law firm whose associates average 2,300 billable hours per year.

The preceding advice may appear self-evident. However, each year many law students mail out reams of résumés and sign up for

as many on-campus interviews as their school permits with legal employers whose track records make it clear that they will not hire the
students in question. These same students also apply to other legal
employers for whom they really have no desire to work, now or in the
future. Whether they do so out of ignorance or fear is irrelevant; in
so doing, they waste valuable time that could be used to target more
desirable legal employers, or to study for their classes. A critical self-
evaluation of the type of legal employer you really want to work for and
the demand for your services will help you to avoid this too-common
pitfall.

Research and Prepare for Job Interviews

Before you go into any interview with a legal employer, you should
do some research. Specifically, you need to find out as much about
that legal employer as possible. What types of law do its attorneys
practice? Does the legal employer have a specialty? How many people
does it employ? Who are some of its key attorneys? Does the legal
employer have more than one office? If so, where are they located?
What clients does the legal employer serve? What is the academic
and professional background of the particular attorney(s) you will be
interviewing with? The more you know about the employer before you
step into the interview, the better it will go.

Besides the NALP Forms, you should also review the *Martindale-
Hubbell Law Directory* listing for the legal employer in question. This
directory contains practice profiles on most law firms and corporate legal
departments, along with individual professional biographies (listing
undergraduate and law degrees, clerkships, publications, bar affiliations,
practice areas, and other accomplishments) for the attorneys who work
for them. Most law libraries keep the *Martindale-Hubbell Law Directory*
at the reference desk.

If you are interviewing on campus, the placement director can
usually tell you the names of the attorney or attorneys who will interview
you. You can also obtain this information by calling legal employers
directly and speaking to the hiring coordinator. (For relatively small-
sized legal employers, interviews may also be arranged by a secretary for
one of your interviewers.) Once you have the name of the interviewer,
look up her professional biography in *Martindale-Hubbell.* Many law
firms also have brochures discussing the firm and containing attorney
biographies to send to potential clients. Ask to see these promotional

materials if you have been invited to interview with such a law firm. In addition, many law school placement offices maintain evaluations of legal employers by former summer clerks from the school. These evaluations can provide frank and insightful information about these prospective employers.

After you have obtained all, or some, of the information referenced previously, utilize it to your best advantage in the interview. For example, if you determine that the attorney interviewing you was an articles editor for her school's law review and you now perform the same task, mention your work as an articles editor during the interview.

Before going to any interview, you also need to prepare by anticipating some of the questions commonly asked. Almost universally, your interviewer will ask why you want to work for his firm or agency. For each employer with whom you interview, have a convincing answer prepared for this question. If, for example, you are interviewing with the legal employer because a fellow law student raved about working for the employer, pass this information along to the interviewer. If you picked this employer because one of its clients recommended it as a good firm, tell the interviewer this. If you have no such personal insight on the employer, at least mention that you were impressed by its narrative statement on the NALP Form (make sure you remember some details though), or that you like its primary practice areas.

Another common question is, "What other legal employers are you interviewing with?" This question is designed to figure out whether you just want a job from anybody, or are genuinely interested in working for the employer of the attorney asking the question. If, for instance, a student tells the interviewer that she is interviewing with 50 possible employers across the country, the interviewer is likely to conclude that the student is not particularly interested in working for him or his company. Accordingly, respond to this question in a way that indicates that you have been reasonably selective in picking legal employers to interview with and that the particular interviewer's firm or employer is at, or near, the top of your list.

Another question commonly asked is, "What do you see yourself doing five years down the road?" Interviewers use this question to help them figure out whether you are willing to commit yourself to their organization for some significant period of time. To a lesser extent, interviewers also use the question to figure out whether you have given any significant thought to the direction your professional career will take. In answering the question, give some indication that you are willing to make a commitment to the right employer, and that you have some goals for the future that are compatible with working for the legal employer considering hiring you.

A common concluding question is, "What questions do you have for me about my firm or organization?" Here, most interviewers are simply trying to give you an opportunity to have your questions about the legal employer answered. They may also be trying to ascertain whether you are able to clearly articulate yourself and be assertive. For these reasons, do not be afraid to ask some tough, but not touchy, questions along the lines of, "Do you enjoy your work? How many years does it take to make partner at your firm? What percentage of associates stay with the firm after two years?" etc.

During the interview, you should also be prepared to discuss the classes you have taken in law school (always a favorite), your past work for other employers, and your legal writing skills. Many legal employers will also want to see one or more writing samples. Accordingly, bring along some high-quality samples whether or not you have been specifically asked to do so. Furthermore, employers will also want to see your law school transcript. Have copies available for the interviewer. If your transcript has a low mark or two, some interviewers may also ask you to explain what happened. Such a question is not a pleasant one to deal with. The best approach is simply to explain what did happen, to indicate that you learned from the experience, and that you (to the extent that such is actually the case) are doing quite well in your classes presently.

Finally, bring several copies of your résumé, transcript, and writing samples to the interview even if you previously supplied them to the employer. The interviewer may not have received them, or may have misplaced them. Being able to provide them on the spot makes the interview more meaningful and makes a good impression.

Present a Good Image

During an interview (and in all dealings with legal employers), it is crucial that you present a good image of yourself. You present such an image by the way you dress and speak, in the materials you provide, and by your conduct and demeanor in dealing with the legal employer.

It may not be fair, but superficial perceptions often do matter even if they are not reflective of your true abilities, so pay attention to details.

An example best illustrates the preceding point. Recently, an attorney one of us knows related that she had received a résumé from a top student from a top law school. However, she did not give the student an interview because his cover letter contained several typographical errors. She figured that if he could not take the time to proofread the cover letter for his résumé, he would not take the time to properly review any work he did for her. This story demonstrates the fundamental principle that all material you give a potential employer should be as perfect as you can make it. This includes cover letters, follow-up letters, résumés, and writing samples.

Other "simple" details are similarly crucial in the interviewing process. When going to an interview, make sure that you arrive for the interview a few minutes early. Getting to an interview late, or on time but out of breath, sweating, and disheveled, makes you appear irresponsible. Dress professionally. Blue or gray business suits are always a safe bet. If you need a haircut before the interview, get it. In short, you need to appear at your best when you meet the interviewer.

During the interview, make every effort to speak clearly and to be personable. (Have a drink of water or coffee if your mouth gets too dry.) Most legal employers use hiring committees to decide who to hire. Often, the person interviewing a candidate assumes (or has been told) that the hiring committee will determine whether the candidate is capable of doing competent work. Such an interviewer is thus mainly interested in figuring out whether he or she could work with the candidate. For this reason, it is important that you appear to be a likable person who is able to listen to and communicate with others. Demonstrate that you are a real person with interests beyond simply studying and writing 50-page briefs. A simple way of showing this is to put some interesting hobbies, interests, or activities that are not law-related on your résumé. Also, remember to occasionally address the interviewer by name during your discussions with him; this adds a personal touch and lets him know you are paying attention.

Be Straightforward and Honest

Many students view looking for a job as some sort of game. It is not. The best approach in dealing with legal employers is to be straightforward and honest. If a particular law firm is your top choice, make sure that firm knows it. If you are willing to accept a firm's employment offer as soon as it can be given, let that be known. If not, apprise the interviewer of that fact and explain why. (Be careful, however, to reaffirm your interest in any offer more than 30 days old. The NALP Guidelines allow an employer to revoke an offer if a student does not reaffirm his interest within 30 days of the offer letter.) Your straightforwardness, if sincere, will be appreciated.

Also, do not under any circumstances misrepresent anything about yourself or your record to a legal employer. "Résumé inflation" in any form is dishonest, unethical, and fraudulent. Presenting false information to an employer may not only prevent you from participating in future interviews with other employers, but could well emerge as a character issue that could prevent your admission to the bar. In short, explain, if necessary, but never deceive.

Network

Your chances of getting a legal job will almost certainly increase if you network. As the term is commonly understood, *networking* means to make contacts with individuals who can in some way help you advance your business or professional career. Sometimes, if you are lucky, such individuals can provide you with direct help; they can offer you a job or purchase your services. Most times, however, such individuals can only supply you with indirect help, but such help is nonetheless valuable—they may know other individuals who can offer you a job or use your services. Individuals who can provide you with indirect job-hunting assistance can be grouped into at least three general categories.

Friends and Relatives: When you are searching for a job, friends and relatives should be kept in mind. We have known law students who have gotten legal jobs, in part, because the students' relatives or friends had connections with legal employers. If you are lucky enough to be in this position, take advantage of it. When you are looking for a job, make sure your friends and relatives know this. Do not assume that they have no job connections of value to you. The only way to find out for sure what connections they have is to ask for their help.

Law School Associates: Not surprisingly, people you associate with at law school often have connections with legal employers. Second- and third-year law students often can provide their peers with good tips about legal employers. Joining one or two student groups at law school can help increase the odds of meeting students with information about employers that interest you. Your placement office can also tell you whether any students at your school have worked for particular legal employers in which you have an interest. Seek such individuals out and discuss your interest.

Your professors can also be a good source for job leads, as well as a source of information about potential legal employers. For example, if you want to work for a firm that specializes in real property law, ask your property professor to recommend such a firm in your area. Most professors are also willing to share their knowledge about the local legal job market with their students if they are politely approached about the subject.

Job Placement Professionals. The value of your law school's placement office and its personnel has already been noted. Other job placement professionals can also assist you. People employed by law firms to coordinate their recruitment of attorneys will obviously assist you when you are seeking a job with their firm. Additionally, these individuals are occasionally willing to meet with law students not interviewing with their firm and to provide them with some general tips for looking for a job in their geographic area.

Usually law firms with 50 or more attorneys employ hiring coordinators to direct their hiring and recruiting processes. If you are having trouble finding a job, you could gain some insight into how to improve your chances of finding work by taking a hiring coordinator to lunch and asking her for some job-hunting suggestions. To obtain such a lunch date, try calling a few big law firms with offices in your area and asking for the recruitment coordinator or director of hiring. Once you get her on the line, explain that you are looking for a legal job and just want general advice as to how to proceed in this job market. Make it clear that you will not pester her firm for a job, but that you simply want to obtain some information. If the person is willing to help, take her out to lunch. (If that is not possible, ask if you can talk to her over the phone about job-hunting tips.) If she is not willing to help, thank her for her time and call someone else.

Recently, third-year law students have also turned to headhunters to help them find jobs. Legal *headhunters* are recruiters who do not work for any particular legal employer, but rather are in the business of finding attorneys for a variety of legal employers as the need arises. They are job brokers and are usually paid a hefty commission if and when they find a lawyer one of their clients wants to hire. (Reputable headhunters do not charge the prospects they are shopping around to various legal employers.) If you find such a headhunter who is willing to shop you around to various employers, there is no reason not to make use of his services. Do not, however, suspend your own independent job search since headhunters are generally only successful in finding jobs for experienced attorneys with relatively unique talents, or who have existing client bases.

How to make contact with individuals that can provide you with direct assistance in your job search is covered in some detail in other parts of this chapter. To be a good networker, however, you should also join one or two groups that have contacts with legal employers. The local bar association for the area where your law school is located is a good example of such a group. Most local bar associations allow law students to join for nominal fees. Getting involved with your local bar association will allow you to learn things about the practice of law normally not evident from your law school classes. It will also provide you with connections and information about legal employers most law students do not have.

You can also network directly with potential legal employers by participating in traditional law school activities. For instance, if you participate in moot court and do well, take the time to introduce yourself to the judges, who are usually lawyers and real judges from the community. These potential legal employers often will be impressed with your advocacy skills and will welcome the chance to meet you on a personal level. If they seem enthusiastic about talking to you, ask them for their business cards. Give them a call if you are interested in working for them at some later date.

Be Aggressive

You need to be aggressive in today's job market. Being aggressive does not mean being rude. Rather, it simply means that you cannot be afraid to pursue leads, to pick up the phone and call strangers who can help you find a job, and to follow through with connections you develop. Most of your fellow students also will be trying hard to find a job. To be successful in your own search, you will need to be at least as aggressive as they are.

Be Flexible

Many law students needlessly restrict their chances of getting a job by announcing to every potential employer that they are only interested in a certain type of practice. Law students who do not want to be litigators (lawyers who go to court to represent clients), for example, often make this mistake. Even if you think that you ultimately want to be a business or transactional attorney who drafts complex contracts, do not tell the firm you most want to work for that you are only willing to do transactional work. If you do, you may not get a job offer from that firm if (as is common today) it does not presently have any openings in its transactional department for first-year attorneys. You also may lose out on a chance to demonstrate to that firm that you are a hard-working and bright individual worthy of receiving an offer to work in its transactional department when an opening subsequently arises.

Other students make the mistake of insisting that they want to limit their practice to a relatively narrow field, like communications law. Others insist that they want to be a lawyer specializing in a dying or waning field, like antitrust law. At least initially, your chances of finding a legal job will increase if you are more flexible about the type of law you are willing to practice. Further, if you do want to specialize, make sure that the area you are interested in is growing, or at least is still a thriving and healthy field. Currently, the following areas of practice, among others, are growing in importance:

- Bankruptcy
- Intellectual Property
- Environmental Law

Stand Out

When asked what one thing he would tell a law student to do to increase her chances of getting a job, an attorney responded that he would tell the law student to differentiate herself from her fellow students. This is sound advice, since legal employers often have a difficult time choosing among numerous qualified applicants.

The time-tested way to differentiate yourself from your fellow students is to get better grades, particularly during your first year. As previously noted, first-year grades, perhaps unfairly, are the most crucial factor among the criteria governing law students' job possibilities.

This is largely because these grades are the only ones available when law students interview for important summer associate or clerkship positions. Comparisons of students based on first-year grades are also easier and arguably fairer than in subsequent years when the curriculum becomes largely elective. Accordingly, you need to make every effort to receive good grades during law school, especially during the first year.

Besides good grades, you can also distinguish yourself from your fellow law students by participating in law review or other legal journals, particularly if you can become an editor. If the legal journal focuses on an area of law practiced by some firms that interest you, so much the better. Success in moot court is also generally considered to be a plus by legal employers. Externships and judicial clerkships also have good résumé value. Some legal employers are also impressed by part-time work experience, especially if other factors are positive.

To increase your marketability, you may also want to consider obtaining a joint degree. For example, if you want to go into the land use field, consider obtaining a joint degree in law and urban planning to distinguish yourself from your peers; if you want to go into business law, consider obtaining an MBA along with your law degree. Most law schools allow their students to participate in joint degree programs, although participating will probably extend your course of study to four years. Furthermore, although such programs usually must be applied to before law school, some joint degree programs accept students after they start law school.

Other options include selecting specific courses that will give you particular skills or knowledge that will be attractive to legal employers. For instance, if you want to work for a firm that practices intellectual property law, take some courses in copyright and patent law. You may also want to take some undergraduate science classes if your law school is connected with a university or college. Most law schools give their students credit for a limited number of undergraduate classes if the classes are related to their legal education.

Another way to gain an advantage in the job market is to become an expert in a certain area of the law. This is not as difficult as one may think. Most law schools offer their students the opportunity to take seminars during the second and third years of law school in selected areas of study. Normally, students enrolled in these seminars are required to research and write a scholarly paper or article for their class grade.

After the paper is written, the student will often know more about its topic than any other person. Try to pick a subject matter for your seminar paper about which little has been written. A paper on a new statute or reported case often fits this criteria. Your professor will also usually be willing to help you find a good topic. Once you decide on a tentative topic, check with your law school librarian to make sure that the article you want to write has not already been published. Also, consider whether the topic will be of interest to legal employers (for example, do not write about Chinese law in the 1800s), since one of the goals of writing the paper is to use it to help you find a job.

After the paper or article is finished, you can further increase your marketability by getting it published. Depending on its length, quality, and content, the article or paper may be suitable for publication as a law review note or comment. Also, consider submitting a condensed version of your paper (just the highlights) to editors of legal magazines or to the local bar newsletter. Such publications are regularly seeking material to fill their pages.

Believe in Yourself

As the old saying goes, if you do not believe in yourself, no one else will. Looking for a legal job, like any other, can be frustrating and humbling, especially in today's tight job market. Some jobs that you really want, you will not get. You need, however, to maintain a positive attitude during your job search and continue on with the hunt in an aggressive and confident fashion.

In summary, though you need to try to get the best grades possible throughout law school to increase your marketability, numerous other ways exist to help you distinguish your résumé from those of your peers. You should, however, be careful not to pursue too many of these other options since almost all legal employers are generally more impressed by the quality of your credentials than by their quantity.

CHAPTER 12

How to Find Legal Employment

"Work keeps at bay three great evils:
boredom, vice, and need."

— Voltaire, *Candide*

Finding that First-Year Summer Job

Finding a law-related summer job after your first year of law school can be extremely difficult, especially in today's job market. Many legal employers simply are not interested in hiring first-year law students because they are too green; that is, they are perceived as not yet experienced enough to do the necessary research and drafting tasks. Employers that are interested usually only hire from the very top of the class. That leaves most first-years shut out from the jobs they may most want. Your main goal at this point, however, should be to gain some job experience that will increase your chances of getting a better job the next summer. Although the NALP Guidelines call for legal employers not to place undue emphasis on first-year summer job experience, employers do consider such experience in evaluating second-year applications.

You can increase your chances of finding a first-year summer law job by following three simple rules. First, start your search early. Do not wait until the month before vacation to begin looking for a job. If you do, you are probably not going to find one, because most law firms decide whether to hire first-years in January, after the fall recruiting season has ended. Thus, start looking before January if you are serious about a summer law firm clerkship. (Under NALP Guidelines, however, first-years are not supposed to contact legal employers about jobs until after November 30 of each year.)

Second, do not be too picky. For example, even if you think you want to be an entertainment lawyer, do not rule out working for a personal injury defense firm during your first summer in law school. Why? Legal experience your first year, no matter what kind, can help you get a much coveted second-year job. Furthermore, after your first year, the area of practice that interests you may well change. The more areas you are exposed to, the better off you will be in terms of making a career choice when law school ends.

Third, consider legal jobs with entities other than law firms, even if you have to volunteer your time. Nonprofit groups such as Consumers' Union or the Center on Law and Poverty often hire first-year law students to work for their legal departments during the summer. Working for such groups will not line your pockets with large sums of money but will provide valuable experience and enhance your résumé. State and federal government agencies or offices also often hire first-year students; for example, do not rule out working for the state attorney general's criminal or civil divisions. One of our colleagues got a job with the California State Attorney General's office (which gave him great experience and helped lead to a later supreme court clerkship) by volunteering his services free of charge. One of us took a summer job after the first year researching for his civil procedure professor, a fascinating and brilliant man with whom he later coauthored a law review article.

Still another option is judicial externships. Both federal and state judges will hire first-year law students to extern with them for a summer. Sometimes these positions are paid, although often they are not. Again, however, they offer good experience and perhaps your first real opportunity to cut your teeth as a future lawyer by working on real legal problems.

Employing the preceding general rules, a concrete first-year summer job-hunting strategy might consist of the following: In December, after your exams are over, consult your law school placement office and make up a list of between 20 and 30 law firms, nonprofit organizations, professors, judges, and government agencies and entities you may be interested in working for the next summer. Most placement offices maintain lists of firms, agencies, and organizations that will hire first-year students. In making your list, try to include some firms or other entities that are not sure to be on everyone else's list.

Next, have your résumé printed up on good bond paper (if you have not already done so) and send it directly to these law firms, agencies, and organizations with a cover letter asking for a summer legal job. Address the letter to the firm's recruiting administrator, hiring coordinator, or other appropriate hiring person. A quick call to the entity you wish to work for can ensure that your letter ends up on the right person's desk. (A sample cover letter and résumé are included in Appendix F.)

In your cover letter, explain why you want to work for the particular law firm or other entity in question. If you want to work for Consumers' Union, for example, you might state that consumer issues interest you, and you have worked for Congressperson X, a well-known consumer advocate. If you want to work for a law firm in Hawaii, you might mention that you were stationed there in the Marine Corps and have an interest in returning to the islands to live after law school is over. In other words, try to include something personal that would appear to make you a good candidate for the specific job you are seeking.

After the letter has been sent, wait a sufficient time for it to be reviewed (a few weeks), then call up the recruiting coordinator or other appropriate person and ask for an interview. This direct approach will not offend anyone, and, to the contrary, it will probably impress its recipient with your drive and initiative. If the organization is interested, it will set up an interview, or else it will honestly tell you that it has not yet reviewed your résumé but will do so in the future.

If you follow the tips in this chapter, you may well end up with some type of legal job your first summer. However, life will go on if you do not. While first-year legal experience is definitely a plus, it is not essential to becoming a good lawyer. Consequently, do not spend an excessive amount of time looking for a first-year legal job. Searching for a first-year legal job should not take priority over doing well in your first-year classes. Good grades will impress a prospective employer during your second year much more than any first-year job you may have had.

If you cannot find a legal job for the summer after your first year, there are also ways to compensate for this lack of experience. One way is to work for a nonlegal employer whose business is related to the type of law you want to practice (for example, a bank if you want to represent financial institutions). Another option for gaining valuable experience is a part-time legal job, whether as a traditional law firm clerk, a professor's research assistant or tutor, or in some other capacity. Such part-time jobs are relatively easy to find and often offer significant legal experience.

The American Bar Association recommends that law students not work during the first year of school. However, a part-time legal job during the second semester of law school may sometimes be worth pursuing as a first-year summer job substitute, provided that it does not unduly interfere with your studies. You can use such a part-time, first-year job to enhance your résumé when interviewing for second-year summer jobs. (Working part time during the second year will normally yield greater experience, but it will be of less résumé value since legal employers interview second-year students for jobs during the fall semester. This is too early for most students to have gained any significant work experience during their second year. This problem can be mitigated to some extent if you can get hired for a part-time legal job while interviewing for second-year summer positions. You can then in good faith represent to potential legal employers that you will have significant job experience when you come to work for them in the future.)

To summarize, it is helpful for your law career and development as a lawyer-to-be to find a summer legal job, so you should expend a reasonable amount of effort to secure such a job. However, you should also consider any such job you are fortunate enough to get as merely icing on the cake, not as an absolute prerequisite to your future success as a lawyer.

Working Part Time during Law School

Should you work part time while attending law school? The answer with respect to the first year is probably not, if you can help it. (Exceptions exist if you need the income to support yourself, or the work complements and does not unduly interfere with your studies.) As discussed previously, the first year is the most stressful and important year of law school, so if you can avoid the distraction and burden of working part time during that year, you should. (Of course, those students attending night law school will normally be working at least part time during their entire period of law study; Chapter 4 addresses the special needs of this growing group.)

For full-time law students, the short answer with respect to working during the second and third years is "it depends." There are a number of issues to consider: your need for additional cash, the value you place on your free time, the alternative uses you have for your time, and the value you place on the experience of working.

Advantages

For most law students, particularly those who have completed the second year, the best wage available is for legal work. Even after your first year, you will have acquired some basic skills that make you valuable to law firms. For example, you will have become familiar with the process of legal research, including the experience of working on computer systems like WestLaw and LEXIS. Also, after your first year, you will have gained some insight into the process known as legal reasoning. You will have a good understanding of case law and precedents and the difference between binding authority and persuasive authority. You will have even received some (not much, but some) instruction in legal writing and will have practiced that skill. You will not be particularly efficient, but from a law firm's perspective, it will be more efficient to use you than to turn a secretary or paralegal loose in the law library, and, for some tasks, it will be more cost-effective than engaging an attorney because your time will cost clients so much less. The bottom line is that a law firm or other legal employer is usually willing and able to pay far more for your time than virtually any other type of employer.

Another advantage of working part time—especially if it is for a law firm—is that it gives you a much better idea of what practicing law is all about. The work you will get as a law clerk will be similar to that of a junior associate in a law firm: conducting legal research and writing memos to partners on the results of your research; helping to draft pleadings, motions, and discovery documents; and assisting in answering discovery. You will begin to get a feel for the nuts and bolts of practicing law. Some jurisdictions even permit law students to make supervised appearances in court, so if your employer is willing and able to provide the opportunity, the possibility exists for getting hands-on courtroom experience.

Even if your jurisdiction does not permit supervised court appearances, you should still have the opportunity to observe attorneys performing in court. This enables you to learn by observing in a situation where you have an interest in the outcome—having helped, perhaps, to draft the very motion that is being heard and argued. The point is that part-time legal work can give you firsthand experience of the day-to-day practice of law before you actually become a lawyer.

This experience is beneficial in several ways. First, you may learn that you really do not want to practice law before you have invested a great deal of time, money, and effort in pursuing a legal career. Or you might change your mind about the areas of law that interest you. For example, entertainment litigation may lose its appeal after you learn that it is just like other litigation, except that occasionally you get to depose people who make movies for a living. (This area of practice generally does not really involve hobnobbing with celebrities.)

Second, you are in a position to benefit by reviewing the work of many different attorneys and by observing them in action. You can learn about things to avoid doing without the pain of learning the hard way by doing them yourself. Additionally, while it can be a bit disillusioning at times, observing other attorneys in action is a great confidence builder. As the realization dawns on you that many attorneys possess mundane intellectual and oratorical abilities, passing the bar exam and successfully making your way in this world will become much less daunting prospects. If these people did it, so can you!

Third, the experience of working part-time gives you a leg up on that summer clerkship following your second year of school. This clerkship is an important step in your career, determining in most cases where your first job as a lawyer will be. It is crucial to make a good impression on your summer employer. Having a good idea of what is expected of you, which can be derived from a part-time job, helps a great deal. Generally, a part-time employer is not very interested, if at all, in impressing you with what a great place its office is to work. The attorneys take a much more utilitarian approach to your work and will let you know what they need and whether your work is helpful. This is not to say that firms do not give summer associates feedback; rather, brutally honest and truly informative feedback is more forthcoming when the evaluator is not concerned about winning the heart of the party being evaluated. Armed with this hard-earned practical experience, you will be in a position to make an especially good impression on your summer (and prospective postgraduate) employer.

The fourth advantage of part-time work, somewhat related to the third, is that it maintains your interest in the law. The old chestnut about law school—the first year they scare you to death, the second year they work you to death, and the third year they bore you to death— contains a fair amount of truth. Working part time gets you interested in a client's case and gives you an incentive to do legal work that may be missing in law school. Wrestling with a knotty legal problem becomes much more important when somebody's money, freedom, or reputation depends on the outcome. Occasionally, some problem from work will intersect with some issue or assignment from school, suddenly making that formerly dreary and seemingly irrelevant course material a lot more interesting. You might even find that your professor is willing to discuss the issue and give you the benefit of his learned opinion. (This might be somewhat touchy, however. Professors, like any other lawyers, are loath to give free legal advice.)

The intersection of schoolwork and part-time work can be particularly fruitful if you are in a clinical program, which is designed to teach the real-world skills of lawyering. Your job then gives you some real-world insight into the course material. This insight makes the course material more familiar and more understandable. It also permits you to get more out of the course than you could have if you did not have some experience with, for example, drafting and answering interrogatories or assisting in preparing for a difficult cross-examination. Having a good understanding of the subject matter enables you to ask meaningful questions.

Conversely, clinical courses provide lots of valuable ideas that you can incorporate (or suggest for incorporation) at work. They are not, however, coterminous with real-world lawyering, and they often suggest a more elaborate method of proceeding with a project than would be practical in the real world. Speaking figuratively of clinicals, the caveat here is that they generally teach you how to build a Cadillac, while in the real world you can often get the job done with (or the client can only afford) a Chevrolet. Practical judgment comes from billing real clients for time spent on real cases.

However, even if you cannot follow the lessons of your clinical course to the letter, the course provides alternative ways of doing things and does so at a stage where you are developing your own system and style of work. Your simultaneous experience in the academic world and the practical world enhances your opportunity to learn and benefits your performance in both.

The fifth advantage of working part time is that you develop an understanding and appreciation for the very important work done by legal support staff. You may be called on to assist in reviewing, organizing, or compiling documents; performing messenger services; or filing documents; among other things. This experience in the nuts and bolts of litigation can be of benefit to you when you become a junior associate with an inexperienced secretary. It also provides you with some firsthand knowledge of the amount of work you will be imposing on your nonattorney staff should you decide to file a 30-page brief with 18 exhibits at the last minute before a filing deadline. The fact that your job duties as a law clerk may overlap with legal secretaries, messengers, and paralegals should cause you to appreciate these individuals more when you become a self-important junior associate attorney. If you are smart, you will let that appreciation manifest itself in professional, courteous, and polite interaction with your valuable support staff, which will benefit both you and those with whom you work.

Disadvantages

The disadvantages of working part time are fairly obvious. You will be spending a certain amount of time working rather than doing other things, such as studying for your classes. Moreover, although your hours will be flexible, by the very nature of the legal profession, at times your job will demand more of your time than you would rather give. To the extent that the time demands of work are unpredictable, working will create difficulties in pursuing other law school activities. For example, working part time and working on a law review will create scheduling problems, if not outright conflicts. Viewed optimistically, this can be advantageous if it forces you to manage your time well, but it also results in a certain amount of stress that you might want to avoid.

Since working part time will definitely limit your ability to participate in other activities, you must balance the benefits you expect to derive from working against the benefits of the activities you will have to forego or curtail. Among those activities is studying your course material. This is not to say that working will make you get lousy grades. However, recognize that working will limit the amount of time and mental energy you will have available to put into schoolwork. If graduating at the top of your law school class is very important to you, you might not want to work part time if you do not have to.

Another disadvantage of working part time is that it limits your freedom as a student. Part-time work forces you to be responsible to and for other people. This runs somewhat contrary to your situation at law school, where you are generally only responsible for yourself. As a student, you generally do not have to answer to anyone for your actions, except to the extent that a professor may give you a poor grade; even then, you are the only one injured by your exercise of poor judgment. Once you begin a part-time job, however, you do have to answer to someone, and other people are profoundly affected by the judgment you exercise.

These added responsibilities will, of necessity, force you to forego certain fun activities that you could previously have engaged in as a more carefree law student. For instance, if you are obligated to burn the midnight oil to help crank out a last-minute reply brief on the same day a truly great party is scheduled, you will have to forego the party or lose your job. In other words, a part-time legal job will limit your freedom, especially the freedom to occasionally do irresponsible things, which is one of the hallmarks of being a student. Therefore, if you want to cherish and enjoy your last moments as a student, taking on a part-time job may not be the best decision for you.

Thus far, we have deliberately omitted discussion of the résumé value, if any, of part-time legal work. Some employers do not consider it at all. Others give it a fair amount of weight. It probably depends on whether they worked part time in law school. Most employers tend to notice it in terms of heightening the importance of other accomplishments; in other words, a student who receives high grades without the added responsibility and time pressure of a part-time job will not be looked upon as favorably as one who achieves the same grades with the added stress of part-time work.

In sum, the advantages and disadvantages of part-time work must be weighed with your personal values in mind. Working part time is not for everyone, but it can be a rewarding experience.

Obtaining a Part-Time Job

If you decide you want to work part time, the next question is how to go about getting a job. The placement office of your law school is the best resource because lots of local attorneys telephone in their needs for law clerk assistance. Alternatively, a summer job can easily turn into a part-time job if it is in the right location. If you worked out of town, your friends who worked in town can provide you with some contacts. Otherwise, try reviewing the want ads and mailing letters offering your services to local firms.

Pursuing the part-time job is much like pursuing the summer job, except that it is done in a more relaxed manner. Remember that part-time employers are looking for hired help, not potential partners. On the other hand, they are not interested in hiring just anybody. In interviewing, always come prepared, dress nicely, try to make a good impression, and be yourself. Once you get the job, show up on time, take care of things you promise to take care of, and do good work. It is that simple.

Second-Year Summer Associate Work

Looking for a second-year summer job is arguably the most important thing you will do during law school. The reason for this is that the type of second-year summer job you obtain and how well you do at it will significantly affect where you work upon graduation. Accordingly, looking for a second-year summer job is not something to be taken lightly.

Because of its importance, you should start preparing for this job search before the start of your third semester of law school. Ideally, you should plan to visit your placement office in late July or early August, before the start of school, so that you can do some research on which legal employers you want to work for and which ones may be interested in hiring you. Use the NALP Forms and other research materials discussed previously for these purposes.

Late July through early August is also a good time to call prospective legal employers directly to informally inquire as to how many people they expect to hire for summer clerkship positions and what types of individuals they are looking for to fill these positions. This period is also ideal for preparing or updating your résumé and identifying good writing samples. If you found a summer job after your first year, you may want to use one of your written projects from that job (being careful to preserve any client secrets or confidential information, of course). Memoranda and briefs you drafted in your legal research and writing class can also serve as good writing samples. (If necessary, you should also revise the sample to correct any grammatical mistakes or typographical errors contained therein.)

It cannot be stressed enough that you should not wait until school starts to identify promising legal employers or to prepare your résumé. The first semester of your second year of law school will be one of the busiest times of your life. Studying for second-year classes and interviewing for second-year summer jobs consumes a huge amount of time. Additionally, many second-year students become involved in such extracurricular activities as law review and moot court; others begin working part time. Thus, you simply will not have enough time to investigate legal employers adequately if you wait until school begins.

Once you have identified somewhere between 30 and 40 prospective legal employers, follow the general job-hunting tips discussed in the preceding chapter. Make sure that you devote your energies to getting hired by legal employers you want to work for and whose past track records indicate that they may be interested in extending you an offer. Under the NALP Guidelines, a prospective employer is required to leave job offers to law students extended in the fall open until December 15, provided that the student reaffirms her interest in the offer within 30 days of the date of the offer letter. If the law student was previously employed by the employer, the NALP Guidelines call for a November 15 deadline.

Hopefully, you will receive one or more job offers. When you receive an offer, immediately send the legal employer a letter confirming your interest in the position and explaining that you will get back to the employer with a firm response to the offer as soon as possible, but no later than the NALP Guideline date. Depending on how strong your interest is in working for the employer extending the offer, you may want to cut back on your interviewing. It is generally a good idea, however, to at least explore the possibility of working for another employer.

Some legal employers will let you split up your summers, working for one employer during the first half and another during the second half. However, such an arrangement usually will not be in your best interests. In deciding which students to offer permanent jobs, most employers will (all things being equal) extend offers to those students who have spent the most time working for them. Such students will be more familiar with the decision-making principals of the employer and may be perceived as more loyal and dedicated to that employer. Thus, if you split your summer, while you may have theoretically increased your chance of getting one permanent job offer, in reality you will probably have to perform significantly better than your fellow summer associates at each workplace to obtain an offer.

After you accept your job offer and show up for work on the first day, there are some key principles to keep in mind.

1. Plan to work hard from the start. First impressions count heavily in determining which students ultimately get permanent job offers. Continue to work hard as the summer progresses, assuming that you are being continually scrutinized.

2. Each legal employer will generally have a certain format or style for the work its employees generate. Normally the preferred format or style is set forth in a procedure manual. If you are given such a manual by your employer, read it thoroughly and do your best to apply the information set forth therein.

3. Attempt to do well on each and every project you are given throughout the summer. Do not try to figure out which attorneys have more input into the hiring process than others and adjust your efforts accordingly. Often it takes a negative comment from only one attorney to prevent a summer associate from getting a permanent job offer.

4. After you finish each project, ask the assigning attorney whether she was satisfied with your work. If she tells you that it has some problems, offer to correct them and do so promptly. In other words, make sure that every attorney you work for is satisfied with your final work product.

5. Participate in the social events your legal employer has for its summer employees. This will help you develop social relationships with the employer's attorneys and your peers. Such relationships will enable you to determine whether you want to work for the employer in the future, and also will help you to know people from whom you can seek much needed advice when a question arises. (Do not overdo the socializing, however, since the bottom line for most employers is how good your work is, not your play.)

6. Do not make the common mistake of taking on too much work, particularly toward the end of your summer job. What counts for summer work is the quality of the product, not its quantity. One summer associate two of the authors worked with got a

permanent job offer even though she spent virtually her whole summer working on a single, complex project. If you take on too much work, you will run the risk of having to leave your job with some of the projects being incomplete or poorly done. Few things upset an attorney more than having work he had previously delegated to another given back to him unfinished or not even started.

The First Permanent Job after Law School

When your second-year summer job is finally over, ascertain how long it will take the employer to let you know if you will receive a permanent job offer. Most legal employers wait until school starts to give out full-time job offers. While you are waiting to hear from your summer employer, do some advance planning in case the news is not positive. Specifically, sign up for interviews with legal employers who are interviewing third-year students on campus. Also, send your résumés and cover letters to other legal employers you would like to work for but who are not interviewing on campus. In doing so, you should recognize that it may be difficult to get a legal job immediately if you do not receive an offer from your summer employer. Accordingly, do not be overly selective in terms of whom you interview with for a legal job after law school until you know for sure that you have at least one permanent offer.

If you do get an offer from your summer employer or another firm or agency, take some risks. If you can arrange it, interview with your "dream" legal employer. At this point, there is simply no reason not to do so.

If you do not get a job offer from your summer employer, do not despair. You should, however, find out why you did not receive an offer. It may simply be the case that the employer had too many qualified applications from which to choose. If this is the case, it is more than likely that the employer will be willing to make some informal efforts to help you find a job. You should, in fact, ask for such help. Even if your summer employer did not give you a job offer because of some perceived deficiencies, chances are one or two of the attorneys you worked for liked you and your work and informed you of this fact before you left for school. Ask these attorneys for whatever help they can give you in searching for a job. Among other things, you should get a letter of recommendation from the attorney(s) in question.

Third-year law students without a job offer may also want to consider working as a contract attorney after law school. Most legal newspapers have want ads for such jobs. Usually, contract attorneys are hired to work on specific cases and for a set duration of time. After the duration is over, the job ends. However, working as a contract attorney can help you gain valuable experience. It may also get your foot in the door of a firm you want to work for on a more permanent basis. Finally, working as a contract attorney also allows a graduating student who has passed the bar, but who does not yet have a permanent job offer, to pay his bills without accepting work from an employer he is less than eager to work for.

Another option for students without offers is to work as a research attorney for state trial court judges. In this way, you can learn a tremendous amount about everyday practice. These positions are not highly sought after, particularly in comparison to the clerkships with federal courts and state appellate courts. Thus it may be possible for you to obtain such a position even if other clerkship positions are already filled.

It is also still theoretically possible for a graduating law student to immediately start working for herself after she passes the bar. Generally though, this is not a good idea because the realities of everyday practice are far different from law school. The costs of starting up a law office (for example, computer equipment, law books, rent, staff, etc.) are also quite high, especially for a new graduate with little cash. However, if you decide to work for yourself, either out of choice or necessity, you can probably find at least a few other lawyers to share the costs associated with running a law practice so as to make it economically possible for you to earn a living.

Professional Publications, Inc. • Belmont, CA

CHAPTER 13

Judicial Clerkships

*"The aim of law is the maximum gratification
of the nervous system of man."*
— Learned Hand, former Judge,
U.S. Court of Appeals, *Time,* May 5, 1958

In addition to other employment opportunities, most law students ponder, at one time or another, the possibility of a judicial clerkship. A judicial clerkship is a position of limited tenure (usually one or two years) as the *law clerk* or *elbow clerk* of a judge, and it is traditionally filled by a recent law school graduate. Law clerks assist judges in the researching, writing, and reasoning tasks that are integral to the judicial function.

Law students may want to become law clerks for many reasons. A clerkship with a judge on a prestigious court (such as the U.S. Court of Appeals) is regarded both as a professional plum awarded to academically distinguished applicants and as a priceless learning experience. Clerks work within courts as insiders and gain a perspective few lawyers will ever share. One of us had the privilege of spending his first year as a lawyer serving as one of California Supreme Court Chief Justice Malcolm M. Lucas' law clerks and agrees that such an experience is invaluable.

Whether a judicial clerkship is something you want to pursue is, of course, up to you; in keeping with our philosophy, however, we hope that this chapter will contribute to making that choice an informed one. Most law students hear about clerkships from their fellow students or professors but have little conception of what clerks do. They may wonder at first what all the clerkship fuss is about.

There are many factors in the clerkship mix. Professors have a vested interest in promoting clerkships among young scholars because an increase in the number of such clerkships obtained by a law school's alumni means an increase in the school's prestige. Judges hope to attract the best and brightest law clerks to help them, and they regularly advertise such positions at the top law schools (which, in this context, always seem to include the judge's own alma mater). Student motivations include obtaining the perceived "write your ticket" plum a clerkship represents, as well as the more noble desires to water the thirsty mind at an intellectual oasis and to help shape the law of the land. For whatever reasons, top clerkship spots are highly prized and are the subject of intense competition among top law students.

What law clerks actually do depends on both the position of the judge they serve and that judge's personality and individual preferences. The subject matter jurisdiction of the judge's court will determine the nature of his work and the weight of his case load. The judge's willingness to delegate will also determine what his clerk actually does.

Trial Court Clerkships

Trial courts that provide clerkship opportunities include the federal district courts, federal bankruptcy courts, the federal court of claims, and state trial courts of general jurisdiction. Federal district judges usually have two law clerks, and federal magistrates and bankruptcy judges usually have one. The number of law clerks hired by state trial judges varies.

A trial judge's law clerk will usually have a large and varied caseload, including researching nuts-and-bolts procedural and law and motion issues. As a result, such law clerks are constantly confronted with a mass of factual situations arising from numerous disputes. As a now-retired federal district court judge once put it to one of us (who was then in his chambers as a young clerkship interviewee), "This is the trenches."

Because of the crushing workload of courts of first resort, trial court judges must be able administrators, and they desire skilled, practical, and efficient clerks to match. The trial court, closest to the everyday world of the practicing litigation attorney, is an "action" place where "the law" and "justice" are meted out daily in the form of dozens of orders, judgments, and decrees.

The clerk or staff attorney must rapidly research the law for controlling statutes and precedents, and he must also consult his common sense and weigh the cases' facts to quickly advise the judge on the exercise of her authority and the limits of her discretion. Should the injunction issue? Have the procedural requirements been met? Which side is telling the truth? Does the court have jurisdiction? What law is the court bound to follow? Though a great many issues recur, the variety is potentially endless, and the depth of the legal research possible is severely limited by large caseloads and other time constraints.

The work of a clerk or staff attorney for a trial judge is certainly important and challenging, but it is not viewed as particularly prestigious (though this is less true in the federal system, where district court clerkships are increasingly sought after). Appellate court clerking is more often associated with distinguished or famous jurists such as Benjamin Cardozo or Oliver Wendell Holmes. Consequently, trial courts generally attract fewer top-caliber law graduates to clerkship positions than do appellate courts.

Appellate Court Clerkships

Appellate courts (especially the U.S. and state supreme courts) and federal courts of appeal are considered the most prestigious places to clerk. Theoretically, these courts deal with fewer cut-and-dried legal issues (because these are resolved at the trial level) and instead decide more important questions of law.

The unfortunate tendency of far too many attorneys to waste their clients' money appealing every adverse decision, however, has contributed to the divergence of practice from this theory. Intermediate state appellate courts with mandatory jurisdiction of appeals are plagued with calendars swelled with both the sublime and the mundane. This overwhelming workload, among other factors, has led many state appellate courts to be perceived as having a high-volume, relatively low quality of output. This, in turn, has diminished the prestige associated with clerking for these courts.

By contrast, because of the limits with respect to federal question and diversity jurisdiction, the variety and complexity of federal court cases, and the position of the U.S. Courts of Appeals themselves as the penultimate tier in the federal judiciary (one step below our nation's highest court), federal appellate court clerkships are highly prized.

Consequently, they are especially difficult to obtain. Federal court of appeals judges usually have three law clerks.

Clerking for the U.S. Supreme Court is obviously the most highly prized clerkship position. Frequently, a clerkship for a Supreme Court justice follows a clerkship for a federal court of appeals judge. For example, a law clerk for a judge on the second circuit court of appeals may graduate upon completion of that clerkship to a clerkship for a justice of the U.S. Supreme Court.

Competition for state and federal supreme court and federal court of appeals clerkships is keen, with grades and academic accomplishments playing a major role. As a rule, only students in the top 10–15 percent of their law school classes need apply; even then, such grades alone will probably not suffice. However, a student lacking stellar marks might compensate with other accomplishments (such as law review editor) if the applicant is bright, hardworking, and a good interviewee with good references. Judges and justices from these courts are looking for (and can command) the cream of the crop with respect to both law schools and individual applicants.

Clerking for an appellate court, especially a court of last resort, provides the rare opportunity to apply one's own talents, legal abilities, and insights to resolving cases presenting difficult and highly important legal issues for precedent-setting disposition. Supreme court cases are landmark cases, chosen for review by the highest court not just to do justice in the individual case, but to shape the law and provide guidance to litigants and other courts in complex and unsettled areas. They can, of course, do so only through resolution of the particular disputes litigants bring before them. In contrast to the trial and intermediate appellate court clerk's orientation of "What is the law I am bound to follow and how does it apply here?" the supreme court clerk's orientation is often more philosophical and policy-oriented: "What should the law be?" The clerk and his judge must often wrestle with conflicting principles and countervailing policies (whose application will often have unclear or uncertain ramifications) to arrive at a decision.

There are some unique opportunities offered by the less-prestigious (but more easily obtained) state appellate court clerkships. In California especially, a variety of factors have severely increased the supreme court's workload and backlog such that it declines to decide many more cases than it previously did. The result of this supreme court logjam is that the courts of appeal have *de facto* assumed a greater role as law- and policymakers than ever before. While legal scholars have bemoaned this abdication of responsibility (especially acute in civil law matters), it presents both a pressing need and a worthwhile opportunity for bright students seeking court of appeal clerkships. Such positions are thus extremely important and should perhaps be given more consideration than they have been in the past by clerkship candidates.

For more detailed and accurate descriptions of judges and clerkships at the courts discussed previously, as well as thoughtful comment on clerkships as an Anglo-American jurisprudential institution, the authors recommend reading *Law Clerks and the Judicial Process* by University of California, Davis law professor John B. Oakley and former California Court of Appeal Judge Robert S. Thompson. Ultimately, your own preferences, not perceived prestige, should determine the type of court for which you would like to clerk.

Personal Factors to Consider

Will you enjoy the research and memoranda- and opinion-writing tasks of a law clerk? If you have never liked writing and researching, a clerkship is not for you. If you do, however, and if you have the grades and desire, clerkships offer an exciting academic experience for you to enjoy before leaving (perhaps forever) the world of academia for the world of private practice. A one- or two-year clerkship could be the ideal transitional job. However, as a government job, it probably will not pay nearly as much as you could command in the private-practice job market, so be certain that your financial status permits you the luxury before committing.

Also, be flexible with your relocation plans if you really want a clerkship because you will probably have to be willing to travel. Clerkships are scarce, and in applying to different judges you should take into consideration the court's geographical location. Would you move to Florida for a federal court of appeals clerkship? Anywhere out of state? How about for a federal district court clerkship? Judges in more popular areas, such as San Francisco or New York, have their choice of applicants from the best law schools in the country. Consequently, it is easier to obtain a clerkship in a less popular area.

Obtaining a Clerkship

If, after taking into serious consideration your qualifications, apti-
tudes, desires, career plans, finances, and short-term residency plans,
you decide you want a clerkship, you have some homework to do. Once
you have narrowed the field of courts for which you would be willing to
work, review the profiles of judges from those particular courts. Decide
whether any exhibit exceptional backgrounds that either attract you to
or repel you from the thought of working for them. Although political
affiliation should not really enter into the picture, compatibility and a
comfort level with the judge you will work for is important.

Work through your school's clerkship committee (if it has one) and
solicit advice from the professors comprising it. Find out their views
of particular courts, locations, and judges. A clerkship committee will
help in many ways to guide you through the clerkship application
process. It will facilitate the forwarding of your transcripts, recommendations, and writing samples, and may even compose a letter to the
judges highlighting your outstanding qualifications and abilities.

If you take advantage of a clerkship committee's services during your
clerkship quest (which we highly recommend), scrupulously observe its
rules. One common rule is that applicants accept the first clerkship
offer they receive so that judges will not be left hanging (unavoidable
pun) while accepted applicants wait for a better offer. This is only fair,
and it has the salutary effect of forcing a clerkship applicant to think
through his choices of court, judge, and location rather than proceeding
in a shotgun approach that unnecessarily defers these crucial decisions
until later.

If you decide to pursue a judicial clerkship, you should be aware
that the application process begins earlier than you would probably
expect. For federal clerkships, students usually send out their résumés
in January or February of their second year. Federal judges generally
hire their clerks during the spring, although some prolong the decision-
making process into the summer. State court judges vary in the timing
of their decisions, and your school's clerkship committee should be able
to provide you with the relevant deadlines. Alternately, you may call
the judge's chambers and ask one of the present clerks.

Finally, a little luck is necessary to get a desired clerkship. Interviews are often the applicant's proving ground—the process by which
the judge decides from among candidates with comparable credentials.

Some judges delay their decisions on which applicants to interview. Accordingly, if you get an interview with a judge in a particular city, you may want to call the chambers of the other judges in that city to whom you have submitted applications to request interviews while you are in the area.

Success in interviews depends on articulateness, maturity, and a great many other intangibles. Be honest, enthusiastic, and relaxed, but above all, be yourself. The interview is also your opportunity to learn as much as possible about the judge and the clerkship, such as the work load placed upon clerks, the level and type of responsibility given to clerks, and what type of travel (if any) is involved in the job. The judge's present law clerks are additional sources of information on these issues.

Clerkships are obviously not for everyone, but they do offer an extremely worthwhile learning experience that is increasingly sought after by the most outstanding law students. A vast number of prominent law professors and attorneys began their careers at the elbow of a judge. At its best, a clerkship will embody the traditional ideal of active interchange between a seasoned, experienced judge and a bright, talented young lawyer short on experience but long on enthusiasm, ambition, legal theories, and ideas. Therefore, if a clerkship of some kind is a realistic possibility for you, by all means give it some serious consideration. Think through your short- and long-term career goals, study the judges and their courts, and solicit advice from lawyers and professors whose judgment you trust. Then follow your instincts and desires.

Professional Publications, Inc. • Belmont, CA

PART 5

The Bar Exam

Chapter 14: Studying for and Taking
the Bar Exam

Studying for and Taking the Bar Exam

*"For the thing which I greatly feared is come upon me,
and that which I was afraid of is come unto me.
I was not in safety, neither had I rest, neither was I quiet;
yet trouble came."*

— Job, Chapter 3, lines 25 and 26

Perhaps no other exam has quite the mystique of the bar exam. It is the ultimate right of passage for lawyers, an intellectual version of fraternity Hell Week, a tribal test of adulthood. The exam, which (in California) is 18 hours long and spread over three days, requires eight weeks of intensive review following three grueling years of law school. The bar exam is indeed something unique and more than a bit daunting, especially considering the surprisingly low passage rates of its highly educated takers. Nevertheless, with proper preparation and the right attitude, the bar exam need not be feared and can instead be considered just another necessary step in your legal career.

As a law student aspiring to become a lawyer, you should view the bar exam as another milestone among many (for example, the LSAT, acceptance at a law school, successful completion of first year, etc.). It is something to be aware of (but not to dwell on) and to confront and overcome at the appropriate time. While the test is certainly no pushover and requires intense preparation, it is not the monster some would have you believe.

One of the most important things you can remember about taking the bar is that everyone in your class statewide (and, in a more general sense, nationwide) is in the same boat. No one taking the test has any advantage except that which they create for themselves through proper preparation. As far as the Board of Examiners is concerned, when test time comes, all Juris Doctors stand equal before the bar with respect to the administration and grading of this anonymously taken exam. And when test time is over, all takers feel equally wiped out and unsuccessful, and all will have to wait for countless months to know whether their pens and pencils worked the necessary magic for them to become, at last, lawyers.

One of the most basic truths about the bar exam is that worrying about it will not help. Other than lining up an appropriate bar review course to take the summer following your graduation, you should not even think about the exam until that course starts. You have enough to worry about during law school without needlessly accelerating bar stress. You are in law school to learn not just specified subject matter, but an entirely new way of thinking and analyzing problems. The bar exam should not exercise an inordinate degree of power over your psyche or your study schedule. Do not even open a bar review book (unless out of curiosity or in search of help with a problem arising in the course of your other studies) until after you graduate and begin formal review.

In no event should you begin studying for the bar exam too early. Starting to study too far in advance is often a direct result of forgetting the most basic truth: You should not worry about the exam (or at least not before its time). Jumping the gun on bar study will lead to worrying and burnout, and you will not be able to retain what you read. It also will reduce or eliminate your precious leisure time for nonlaw activities and distract you from more important legal work as well (such as finishing your law review article, preparing for classes, outlining, or studying for midterms or finals).

One of us, as a second-year law student working assiduously to become a law review editor, witnessed a case in point. A third-year law student at his school began studying and reviewing for the bar exam (held in late July) in January. This student, although a law review editor and a seeming cinch to pass the bar but for his neurosis over the test, ended up flunking the exam the first time around despite his five-month jump on his classmates (the great majority of whom passed). Far from ensuring success, his behavior produced undue worry and anxiety and was otherwise unproductive.

Premature studiers are often excessive studiers; such study fanatics worsen their plight by not taking time out even to care for themselves or to remedy fatigue. Treat yourself well during bar study, making sure to get plenty of exercise and sleep. Do not work during this time unless absolutely necessary. Pamper and nurture yourself. If possible, take a vacation right after graduation for a week or so to clear your head and prepare yourself mentally for the arduous eight weeks of intensive review that lay ahead.

It is not easy to cram the most important parts of three years of law study into eight short weeks (which is why a formal review course is indispensable). If you want to be at your best, you need to be physically and mentally fit and fully alert. Think of yourself as a boxer preparing for a championship fight. While you must work long and hard, putting in every mile of roadwork and sparring every round, you must not overtrain. Skipping meals, losing sleep, and worrying excessively will render you vulnerable come fight day no matter how relentlessly you drive your body.

Assuming you have graduated, enrolled in a reputable bar review course (such as BarBri), regularly attended lectures, and studied in the right frame of mind, nothing should prevent you from giving your best performance on the exam, which will usually be more than enough to pass. Bar review courses combine massive written materials (including practice tests and outlines similar to the kind law school has already acquainted you with) with a series of videotaped (and sometimes live) lectures. The format is similar to that of law school—minus the Socratic element, of course. However, the range and pace of study are more intense and the level of analysis is by necessity more broadbrush. You will cover over a dozen major areas of law in a comprehensive (if not detailed) fashion in a mere eight weeks. Though this may seem daunting and may tempt you into making the fatal error of early study, do not succumb. Most or all of the material should be familiar from your law school curriculum, thus easing the burden and anxiety.

Studying for the bar exam is, in a way, like becoming reacquainted with old friends. Viewed in this light, it can be a very positive, uplifting experience. Further, it should serve to build rather than decrease your confidence because you will be amazed at how much law you already know.

Nevertheless, do not expect all candy and flowers. The review course will be hard work, and you may feel like screaming after having taken your second practice test and read your third outline of the day. Because of the review's intensity, we reemphasize that students preparing to take the bar exam should not work if at all possible. Many employers offer stipends to offset in whole or part the costs of reviewing for and taking this rigorous but necessary test.

Once you begin bar review, the basic tenets of hard work and good sense that got you into and out of law school will serve as fine guides. Stick to the course program faithfully and be sure not to fall behind— eight weeks is very little time considering the range of materials that must be covered.

Although you will be deluged with an assortment of different extras allegedly designed to improve your performance and increase your chances of success on the "big test," exercise a cautious restraint. If it is really in your best interests to take a supplemental course on essay writing, multistate multiple-choice test-taking strategy, or performance exam skills, by all means take the course or courses if you have the time, money, and energy. If, however, the practice tests you are taking indicate you are doing just fine and have no special weaknesses in any of those areas, do not fall prey to propaganda or paranoia that might ultimately cost you in terms of fatigue and burnout. In other words, follow the age-old maxim: "If it ain't broke, don't fix it." Followed faithfully, the standard bar review regime is taxing and challenging enough, and it should prove to be a thoroughly adequate review for the great majority of students.

It is best to purge your social calendar of major events during the period of your bar study. Do not be antisocial, just extremely flexible. Do not plan any major events like weddings, weekend fraternity reunions, extended trips, or anything else that would impair your ability to study when and as needed. This does not mean you should hole up in your tiny apartment, store up a cache of food, paper your walls with outlines, and lock yourself in—far from it. As discussed previously, if you take a fanatical "study till I drop" approach, you will most likely burn out, decrease your absorption and retention, and increase your chances of failure.

Regular exercise and healthful, regular meals will help ensure that you do not experience mental fatigue. These respites from the grind of studying also provide welcome arenas for mentally refreshing nonlegal conversation with friends and family. It is important to be mentally and physically fresh and prepared for the bar exam; you do not want to be a nervous wreck or sidelined with a flu or cold that you acquired while burning the midnight oil to the point of exhaustion. You simply cannot pass the test if you are not well enough to take it.

Another important principle that is a key to your success is "Don't procrastinate!" Do not waste time—it is a precious commodity you have much too little of in preparing for the most important test you have ever taken. Take an hour or two out now and then to play handball or run (it will refresh you and decrease your anxiety), but do not hang out afterward for booze and beers, which will consume precious hours and leave you fuzzy-headed, hung over, and unable to perform the important task of studying. Do not put off until tomorrow because during bar study, if you do, you will be one day behind. Try to follow Aristotle's principle of moderation in all things; too much or too little study can prove fatal to your success. Basically, be diligent and responsible, and use the good sense that got you through law school to guide you through the bar review period.

It is also important to maintain a positive attitude throughout your study. Approach the test with the attitude that you will give your best effort and that it will be enough. If you do, it will. Avoid getting down on yourself if you are giving your best efforts. You will not do well on (and this may be a shock) or even pass every practice test you take during the review period. In fact, some review courses purposely grade the initial practice tests by extremely harsh standards to jolt their enrollees into taking the matter seriously. Likewise, there will almost certainly be a point during the actual bar exam when you feel you have failed or done poorly on at least one section. You must put aside this feeling, realize that all bar takers feel the same way, and, doing the best you can, finish the entire exam.

Do not harp on failures or gloat about successes. It will all average out in the end and one practice test will not make or break you. Work on improving your weaknesses and maintaining your strengths. Hang out with friends who are serious students, not blowoffs or pessimistic naysayers who will bring you down and make you doubt your ability or purpose. Also, to further the end of fostering mental balance and a positive attitude during this trying time, avoid hopelessly neurotic classmates at all costs; study peacefully by yourself if that is the only feasible alternative.

As your formal bar review draws to a close, you should begin to see the big picture and your preparedness should be peaking. Develop a study plan for the final few days before the test and mark your calendar accordingly. If you have followed the preceding program and faithfully (though not fanatically) studied all the materials provided, you should approach the final few days with minimum anxiety and maximum confidence. You will be satisfied you have absorbed as much as you are capable of and as much as you will need to pass, and you will view the last few days as a tune-up, to be spent reviewing your capsulized outlines and perhaps working on a few sample problems.

If you are confident that you are well-organized and current in your studies, you may even want to skip the final few scheduled lectures and follow your own study plan to avoid exposing yourself to the "nervous Nellies" you will begin to encounter among your less-disciplined class-mates. If you choose this option, you can make special arrangements to listen to the taped lectures you will miss in advance.

After you have prepared the best way you know how for the test, reinforce your sound perspective of the whole process by reminding yourself once again that it is only a test, that the worst thing that can happen to you is that you will fail it and have to take it again, and that many fine lawyers practicing today have done just that. Your essence and identity are not wrapped up in passing an exam (if they are, they should not be). Having put forth your best efforts to prepare for the test, and having accepted that the worst-case scenario is nowhere near the end of the world, be calm and confident. Know that the statistics are on your side (and, if they are not, that your excellent preparation is the unknown variable) and that you will succeed. After all, you do not have to ace the bar exam; you just need to pass it. So be calm, confident, and alert, but not cocky. Cockiness and overconfidence can prove fatal to success if they lead to underpreparedness.

As the date of the exam approaches, leave nothing regarding the mechanics of the actual exam to chance. Plan your rides to and from the testing area, your living quarters during the test (perhaps a hotel if the drive is too far), and whether you will stay on or leave the test premises for meals during lunchtime. Make sure you have enough pens, pencils, erasers, timekeeping devices, and whatever else you need for the test. Finally, if you have prepared properly, you will not need it, but "Good luck!"

Appendices

Appendix A: Formal Brief

Appendix B: Course Outline

Appendix C: Course Mini-Outline

Appendix D: Class Flowchart

Appendix E: Sample Exams

Appendix F: Résumé and Cover Letter

Formal Brief

This appendix contains a sample formal brief. Briefing cases for class is discussed at the beginning of Chapter 7.

Masterson v. Sine (1968) 68 Cal2d 222

Facts and Case History

Mastersons sold their ranch to defendants Sines on 2/25/58. The grant deed reserved "unto the grantors" an option to repurchase the ranch on or before 2/25/68. The repurchase price was to be the "same consideration as being paid heretofore plus the depreciation value of any improvements. . ." Mr. Masterson was subsequently adjudged bankrupt, and his spouse and the bankruptcy trustee (plaintiffs) sued for declaratory relief to establish their right to exercise the option.

Plaintiffs contended the repurchase price language meant $50,000 (i.e., initial purchase consideration) plus the value of improvements by grantees. Defendants contended the option language was too uncertain to be enforceable and extrinsic evidence (evidence outside the grant deed itself) was inadmissible to show its meaning. Defendants also contended the option was personal to the grantors and was thus not enforceable by the trustee because the parties had intended the property to be kept within the Masterson family. (Mrs. Sine was Mr. Masterson's sister.)

The trial court granted judgment for plaintiffs declaring the option enforceable. Defendants appealed and the judgment was reversed by the Supreme Court.

Holdings

(1) Parole evidence was properly admitted to explain the meaning of the unclear language concerning the repurchase option price in the grant deed.

(2) Parole evidence also should have been admitted to show an alleged collateral agreement that the grant deed's repurchase option was exercisable only by the grantor because the grant deed contained no integration clause and the alleged collateral agreement was one that might naturally be made by the parties.

Legal Rules

(1) The Parole Evidence Rule: When a written contract is an "integration"— i.e., the complete and final expression of the terms of the parties' agreement—parole evidence (i.e., evidence outside of the document itself) may not be admitted to add to, vary, or contradict its terms.

(2) Corollary and Related Rules:

    (a) Parole evidence is not barred by the parole evidence rule where the contract is not an integration.

    (b) Parole evidence is not inadmissible to explain the meaning of unclear or ambiguous terms in a written document.

    (c) When only part of an agreement is integrated, parole evidence is not barred to prove elements of the other unwritten part.

Legal Reasoning

The court reasoned that the deed contained no integration clause and that its formalized structure was not readily amenable to inclusion of collateral agreements. Further, the court reasoned that the parties were neither experienced in land transactions nor had any warning of the disadvantages of failing to put the alleged collateral agreement in writing. Hence, the agreement was one that might naturally be made separately.

Course Outline

This appendix is a sample course outline, provided as an example of the outlines we suggest that you create during the school year and use to study for your final exams. This outline is for a course in evidence. It illustrates the levels of organization and detail usually appropriate for law school study.

The author of this outline uses phrases and abbreviations; however, you may be more comfortable using complete sentences and spelling out each word. The extent to which you use abbreviations is entirely up to you. Be sure that your abbreviations are not too cryptic to avoid wasting time trying to figure out what your outline means while studying for final exams. Using abbreviations and sentence fragments obviously saves time when writing the outline and makes the outline shorter and easier to review. These benefits should be balanced by the need to be able to understand your outline at a glance.

Following is an explanation of the abbreviations used in this outline.

Δ	defendant
acc	accused
adm	admissible
A&C	attorney and client
b/c	because
b/w	between
c/a	cause of action
c&c	clear and convincing
cnsl	counsel
conf comm	confidential communication
conv	conviction
cross-ex	cross-examination
C	client
CalSCt	California Supreme Court
CCP	Code of Civil Procedure
CEC	California Evidence Code
Ct	court
depos	depositions
D/P	due process
evid	evidence
FF	foundational facts
FRCP	Federal Rules of Civil Procedure
FRE	Federal Rules of Evidence
inadm	inadmissible
ID	identification
L	lawyer
negl	negligence or negligent
opp	opportunity
priv	privilege or privileged
P/C	probable cause

P/O	police officer
rep	representative or reputation
req'd	required
reqmt	requirement
RR	recorded recollection
stmt	statement
suff	sufficient
unavail	unavailable or unavailability
unconst	unconstitutional
USSCt	United States Supreme Court
vs	against
V	victim
w/	with
w/o	without
W	witness

The author of this outline also uses relatively informal structure, distinguishing among sections by using headings and indenting. You may be more comfortable creating an outline with hierarchical numbers—Roman numerals, capital letters, Arabic numerals, lowercase letters, etc. The disadvantage of attempting to impose too much structure on your outline while it is in process is the lack of adaptability. You should maintain adaptability in your outline because your understanding of the course structure will probably change as the course progresses.

Evidence Outline

Relevance

CEC 210/FRE 401—*relevant* means any tendency to make the existence of a fact in dispute more or less likely.

Substantive law and legal elements provide the basis for relevance.

Two types of objections:

Immateriality—the fact itself is irrelevant based on the substantive law.

Irrelevance—the evid offered is not very good proof of the fact sought to be proved

There is a distinction b/w relevant and sufficient evid.

CEC 352/FRE 403—Even if relevant, the probative value can be substantially outweighed by the prejudicial impact—exclude evid.

FRE 407—Subsequent corrective measures are not adm to show negl.

May be adm to show ownership, control, or feasibility of corrective measures (if controverted) or impeachment.

Issue must be in dispute (if not controverted, no evid can make it more or less likely), not relevant.

People v. Ramos CalSCt—If Δ offers to stipulate and give prosecution all proper probative points, prosecutor must stipulate.

If stip doesn't give all possible inferences, should weigh remaining probative value vs prejudicial impact.

Circumstantial Evid

FRE 103—reversible error

Circum evid has a less direct connection to fact sought to be proved than does direct evid—relies upon an inference that the sought fact existed.

Probability proof:

> *People v. Collins* CalSCt—Rejected probability proof because probabilities made up, factors controverted, factors linked.
>
> Also CEC 352 problem of jury overweighing.

Probability—Proof beyond a reasonable doubt/by a prepond has to be proven as to each issue separately.

Distinction b/w:

> (1) Direct evid: If jury accepts evid completely, the fact is established 100%.
>
> (2) Circum evid: If jury accepts evid completely, there is still only a % possibility that the fact existed.

The proponent of the evid bears the burden of proving the underlying assumption.

Flight is indicative of guilt—jury may consider flight.

People v. Montgomery—Nonflight is as consistent with guilt as with innocence.

Opinion Testimony

FRE 602—Personal knowledge reqmt for witness

> May be provided by the witness himself.
>
> Must have evid sufficient to support a finding.

FRE 701—Lay witness opinion must be:

> (1) rationally based on witness' perception; and
>
> (2) helpful to understanding the witness' testimony.

Opinion factors:

> (1) Can witness reduce conclusion to more elemental terms?
>
> (2) Does the conclusion give the jury something they wouldn't otherwise have?
>
> (3) Does the witness have the requisite knowledge to form the opinion?

Underlying facts can be elicited on cross-ex to the extent not req'd for personal knowledge.

Some opinions require expert knowledge.

FRE 704—The fact that the opinion goes to an ultimate issue does not make it objectionable. Although if issue is a legal conclusion for the jury, it is not "helpful" under 701 (b) for witness to testify as to negligence or *mens rea.*

Jury may want both the underlying facts and the opinion (i.e., that someone was drunk).

Generally no best evidence objection.

> CEC 412—If weak evid offered when w/in power of attorney to offer stronger evid, should be viewed w/distrust.

Generally opinion/conclusionary objection is highly discretionary.

Reversible Error

(1) No error committed:

(A) Ct req'd to rule as it did.

(B) Ruling discretionary & no abuse.

(2) Even if error:

(A) No objection below.

(B) Objection lacked specificity.

(C) If objection sustained, offering party can make offer of proof.

(3) Even if error & specific objection, not reversible

Watson—Not reasonably probable that a more favorable result would have been reached w/o the error.

Formal Objections

FRE 611

Leading questions:

Allowed in cross-ex.

Usually permitted as to FF not in dispute.

Permitted when calling adverse party on direct, or witness identified w/adverse party.

Ct has discretion to control examination.

CEC 766—Either party may move to strike as nonresponsive.

Exceptions:

To refresh recollection

With very young or squeamish witness

CEC 776

(a) Adverse party or person identified w/same examined by other side on direct—leading.

(b) Cross-ex by any party by leading questions except:

(1) for a party as witness, by his own cnsl or cnsl for a nonadverse party—no leading.

(2) for nonparty witness, by cnsl of party w/whom witness identified or cnsl of nonadverse parties to party w/whom witness identified—no leading.

(c) Identified w/a party means:

(1) persons for whose immediate benefit action prosecuted.

(2) agent, rep, etc., while entity is a party.

(3) agent, rep, etc., when c/a arose.

(4) agent, rep, etc., when witness gained sought knowledge.

Questions beyond the scope of the preceding examination

Cts have discretion to allow questions beyond the scope.

Character Evidence

FRE 404—Character evid inadm to prove conforming conduct.

Except an acc may offer evidence of a pertinent character trait of his or of the victim.

If acc offers evid, prosecution may offer evid in rebuttal.

Prosecution may show homicide victim's peacefulness.

Character for truth and veracity of a witness.

Methods of Showing Character

FRE 405—Reputation or opinion always OK

On cross-ex inquiry allowed into specific instances.

Specific instances adm if character is essential element.

Specific acts are time-consuming & have danger of overweighting.

What is character evidence?

(1) Lifestyle evidence

(2) Genetic testimony

(3) Psych testimony

CEC 1102 & 1103—draws distinction

Evid of Δ's character by Δ, or by prosec in rebuttal—opinion & rep

Evid of V's character by Δ, or by prosec in rebuttal—opinion, rep, & specific act.

Habit

FRE 406—Habit is relevant to prove conforming conduct.

Habit does not carry moral judgments—less prejudicial.

Habit is semi-auto—almost invariable response to certain stimuli.

CEC 1105—Habit or custom is adm to prove conforming conduct—draws a distinction b/w habit & character.

Evidence of Other Wrongs

FRE 404 (b)

Not adm to show conforming conduct.

Adm to prove motive, intent, etc.

Intent—especially when conduct is undisputed.

Require another connection with the fact sought to be proved than via an inference about the character of the Δ.

Still subject to balancing under FRE 403.

Mental states by their nature must be shown by circumstantial evid.

Adm may hinge on need for the evid—ambiguity of underlying conduct.

Common scheme or plan showing identity

    (1) Degree and distinctiveness of shared features

    (2) Number of minimally distinctive shared features

Preconceived design: connected events leading to goal

Common manner of committing crimes

Standard of Proof *Tucker v. Nevada*

Must show other crime by clear & convincing evidence.

    FRE 404 (b)—Standard of relevance—sufficient to support a finding.

    Jury is free to reject evid if they find Δ did not commit it.

Double jeopardy problem if tried & acquitted of the "other crime."

Might admit b/c c&c or sufficiency are lower standards than proof beyond reasonable doubt.

Credibility

FRE 608—Character for truthfulness of testifying witness

    (1) May come in as opinion or reputation.

    (2) Specific acts may be inquired into on cross-ex:

        As to that witness' credibility

        As to the witness about whom the instant witness has provided credibility evidence

Prior Convictions FRE 609—shall be admitted if elicited from witness himself on cross-ex or established by public record.

    Requires:

        (1) Crime punishable by one year, or

        (2) Crime involving dishonesty or false stmt

CEC 788—Prior felony convictions may be adm.

    Subject to CEC 352—balancing

    Spearman—prior heroin poss conviction

    Balancing:

        (1) Identity of prior conviction w/present charge.

        (2) Inhibiting effect on Δ's ability to testify.

        (3) Prior conv must involve "dishonesty"—necessary element of the offense must be the intent to lie, defraud, deceive, steal.

    Objections to use of prior convictions:

        (1) Double jeopardy

        (2) Left-wing social causation of crime theory

        (3) Naked self-interest of witness will determine.

Prop 8: §28 d—Truth in evidence (leaves CEC 352 alone)

        §28 f—Prior conv shall be used w/o limitation

FRE 609 (a)(1)—Subject to balancing similar to FRE 403, only now tilted in favor of exclusion

> (a)(2)—Not w/in Ct's discretion; convictions come in.

> Asking the witness on cross if he had been convicted under *Michaelson* analogy might have to demonstrate to the court that W had been convicted first.

> Creates possibility of jury misusing the evidence.

CEC 780—List of permissibly considered factors re credibility

Prior inconsistent statement:

> FRE 613 (a)—Witness need not be shown or have the contents disclosed of the prior statement.

> FRE 613 (b)—Prior inconsistent statement inadm unless witness given an opportunity to explain.

> Here only used for negative aspect (destroying credibility of trial testimony), not for positive (prior statements as the truth).

FRE 610—Can't impeach w/religious beliefs.

> Bias may be shown if religious practice identifies the witness with a party.

Constitutional Aspect

> *Davis v. Alaska*—Δ sought to introduce a prosecution witness' juvenile conviction records. USSCt held the bar was unconst denial of Δ's right to confrontation.

Collateral impeachment—the underlying fact is irrelevant but W has lied on the stand.

> Common law permitted cross-ex into collaterals but couldn't introduce extrinsic evid to rebut.

> FRE doesn't specifically address.

> > May apply FRE 608 by analogy & permit inquiry on cross-ex, but no extrinsic evidence (specific instances of conduct for attacking credibility).

> CEC 780 commentary—collateral impeachment within the trial Ct's discretion

Rape Evid

CEC 1103 (a)—Specific acts of V generally adm to show V's char to prove conforming conduct if offered by Δ.

FRE 412 (a)—Opinion or reputation evid re V's past sexual behavior not adm.

> 412 (b) specific acts of V adm:

> > (1) if const req'd.

> > (2) to show Δ not the source of semen/injury.

> > (3) past conduct w/Δ.

CEC 1103 (b)—opinion, reputation, specific act inadm to prove consent:

> (1) Except conduct w/the Δ.

> (2) If prosecution offers evid or V testifies about prior sexual conduct, Δ may cross-ex or introduce limited rebuttal evid.

> (3) CEC 1103 (b)(4)—evid adm to attack the witness' credibility

Screening procedure FRE 412 & CEC 782

In camera exam before evid given to jury

Hearsay

Defined—a statement other than by the witness on the stand offered to prove the truth of the matter asserted therein (FRE 801).

Hearsay problems:

(1) no cross-ex

(2) no observation of declarant by Fact Finder

(3) not under oath

(4) opportunity to impeach lessened

Hearsay risks:

(1) risk of erroneous perception

(2) risk of faulty memory

(3) risk of insincerity (lying)

(4) risk of ambiguity in meaning

FRE 801 (d) statements not hearsay.

(1) Prior statement by witness:

(A) Inconsistent w/testimony & given under oath.

(B) Consistent w/testimony & offered to rebut express or implied charge of fabrication or improper influence or motive.

(C) One of identification of a person after perceiving him (line-up).

Assertiveness required of statement or nonverbal conduct.

Compare nodding head vs saying "ouch."

If not intended as assertion, less risk of insincerity.

Burden is on opponent to show nonverbal evid intended as assertion.

Critical to identify the statement and the declarant.

Statements not offered for their truth.

Legally operative language—defamation, offer, & acceptance

Where content of the statement is not important: "I can talk." The fact that the statement was made is what is important.

P/C inquiry to show facts available to P/O

(1) To show knowledge of a party.

(2) To show statement's impact/effect.

(3) To show speaker's intent.

Hearsay: The statement indicates the declarant's belief in the contents which indicates the truth of the facts.

Nonassertive conduct is very similar in analysis to hearsay although risk of insincerity is much less.

Critics say any conduct, verbal/nonverbal, assertive/nonassertive, if offered to support an inference about the declarant's belief to further support on inference about the truth of the belief, should be treated like hearsay.

Hearsay Exceptions

Declarations against interest.

Unavailability required.

Against interest requirement.

Must be vs interest at time statement made.

CEC 1230—includes penal, monetary, & tending to expose the declarant to hatred, ridicule, social disgrace.

FRE—pecuniary or proprietary or civil or criminal liability

If criminal liability of declarant exculpates a Δ the statement is inadm unless corroborating circumstances indicate its trustworthiness.

Statements might be partly vs interest & partly self-serving. Most Cts do not "sever"—entire statement is in or out.

Personal knowledge requirement:

CEC—explicit reqmt

FRE—implicit reqmt

Statements that are self-serving or vs interest depending on the offerors perspective.

Preliminary Facts (Foundational):

FRE 104 (a)—Ct determines, must be persuaded as to FF before adm—final determination re FF

FRE 104 (b)—Ct admits if suff evid to support a finding

Prima facie standard.

Applies to situations where the relevance depends on the FF.

Ct can't consider inadm evid to determine FF.

FRE 104 (a)—Ct may consider inadm evid, except evid barred by privilege, in determining FF.

CEC 403—prima facie standard (suff to support finding):

(1) Relevance depends on FF

(2) Personal knowledge of witness

(3) Authenticity of a writing

(4) Whether a particular person made the statement or engaged in the conduct

CEC 405—Ct determines under higher standard as to other FF.

Ct is bound by rules of evid in making determination.

If FF is also a fact in issue, the jury shall not be informed of the judge's determination.

FRE 104 (e)—Evid relevant to weight & credibility still adm.

> CEC 406—same as FRE

Burden of proof depends on the legal rule involved.

> If relevance—proponent
>
> If hearsay—opponent
>
> If exception—proponent
>
> If incriminating (5th Am)—witness

Hearing on FF before jury or not:

> (1) can economize if jury would get to hear later on weight & credibility vs danger jury will misuse.
>
> (2) within Ct's discretion, except:
>
> (3) FRE 104 (c)—voluntariness of confession outside the jury

Voluntariness

> *Jackson v. Denno*—Unconst to let jury alone make determination—will not disregard it.
>
> FRE 104 (a) & CEC 405—Judge makes determination & jury can hear on weight & credibility.
>
> Mass—Judge determines but jury can decide to exclude (second crack).
>
> Burden of proof—*Lego v. Twomey*—preponderance

Admissions

Declarant is present in court so hearsay risks diminished b/c w/in his power to set the record straight.

> CEC 1220—Admissions are exception to hearsay.
>
> FRE 801 (d)(2)—Admissions are not hearsay.

Inculpatory/exculpatory character doesn't matter.

Mahlandt—"Sophie bit a child"

> Adm as admission.
>
> Might view as double hearsay "Somebody said Sophie bit a child."
>
> > FRE 805—Need a hearsay exception for each level of hearsay.
>
> Interesting: either double hearsay or single hearsay expressing speaker's belief or opinion.
>
> Judge did not view as double hearsay but expression of Δ's opinion.

Adm vs the organization:

> FRE 801 (d)(2)
>
> > (C) Authorized speaker
> >
> > (D) Agent w/in scope of agency
>
> Agency exceptions don't work the other way.
>
> > Stmts of org not adm vs the agent.

Guilty plea in another case is adm as an admission of each & every element of offense.

Nolo contendre

Coconspirator Exception

FRE 801 (d)(2)—offers a progression:

(A) Statement by party himself

(B) Statement by somebody else adopted by the party by words or conduct

(C) Statement by person authorized to speak for the party

(D) Statement by person as agent w/in scope of agency

"W/in scope" means the subject matter is w/in the scope, not that ability to make stmt us w/in the scope.

(E) Statement by coconspirator during course of aid in furtherance of the conspiracy

Foundation—that conspiracy existed & acc & declarant were members

Determination is made by the judge alone.

Danger of jury misuse

Judge can't consider the statement itself.

Order of proof:

(1) Sequential—independent evid of FF, then the stmt

(2) Flexible—hearsay comes in before determination of FF.

Burden of proof between sufficiency (prima facie) & preponderance.

Problem w/"in furtherance of the conspiracy" reqmt:

If strictly construed, wouldn't need exception b/c all stmts would be legally operative language—not hearsay.

CEC 1223—Deals w/FF under 403—mere sufficiency

CALJIC requires jury to disregard unless they find the FF.

Temporal limits of conspiracy:

Traditional view—ended at arrest

Alt—concealment is part of conspiracy

Past Recollection

Past recollection recorded:

FRE 803 (5)—Writing made or adopted by witness when matter fresh in memory, & reflect that matter correctly.

Commentary indicates two-party proof is acceptable

CEC 1237—Contemplates multiparty recordation & proof.

Writing may be read into evidence but not admitted itself.

Adverse party may offer the evid.

Witness must have insufficient present recollection. Idea is that the hearsay must be necessary.

Past Recollection Refreshed

Leading questions are permissible when the witness has testified to a lack of memory.

Unless offered in evidence, something used to refresh recollection is not objectionable as hearsay.

If witness is just reading the writing (not refreshing recollection), the use is hearsay.

Genuineness of witness' recollection is FF under CEC 403 prima facie test.

Opposing cnsl can offer the recording of the recollection (the writing).

FRE—no explicit reqmt of personal knowledge

FRE 612 & 803 (5)—require a writing

FRE 612—makes writings used to refresh recollection discoverable (except for criminal Δ under Jencks Act)

Prior Identification

Lineup ID more reliable than in-court ID.

801 (d)(1)—Declarant must testify at trial & be subject to cross-ex on the stmt.

Barbati—Ct viewed as chain of custody rather than hearsay—barmaid testified that passer of counterfeit bills was arrested by police. Police testify they arrested Δ.

Present Sense Impressions; Excited Utterance

Statement made contemporaneously is reliable.

No danger of failing memory.

Less risk of fabrication.

Circumstances invite contradiction.

FRE 803 (1)—stmt describing or explaining an event or condition while declarant perceiving it, or immediately after.

FRE 803 (2)—stmt relating to startling event while declarant under the stress of excitement caused by the event.

Availability doesn't matter.

FF—803 (1)—contemporaneous: Declarant perceiving circumstances of stmt & stmt itself considered.

803 (2)—under stress of excitement: event itself & W's perceptions of declarant's excitement

CEC 1240—requires stress of excitement

CEC doesn't have analogue to FRE 803 (1).

If relating to ID may also come in under FRE 801 (d)(1)(A).

Dying Declarations

FRE 804 (b)(2)—unavailability req'd

> Declarant must believe he is about to die.
>
> In Cal. witness has to die.
>
> In civil cases, declarant doesn't have to die.

FF—declarant's belief of impending death

> Declarant's stmts about belief—state of mind exception
>
> Under FRE 104 (a) the stmt itself may be considered.
>
> Stmt must concern cause or circumstances of death under both FRE & CEC 1242.

State of Mind

FRE 803 (3)—State of mind is in issue so hearsay by that person is adm.

CEC 1250—present state of mind

CEC 1251—past state of mind

> No FRE analogue

Reasons for state of mind relevance:

> (1) *Mens rea* in criminal cases or state of mind itself is of legal significance.
>
> (2) To prove future conduct in accordance w/previously expressed state of mind.

Exception to the exception:

> Can't use to prove the facts remembered or believed—"I believe X ran the red light."

Problem arises when declarant's statement also expresses a belief about another person's conduct.

> *Alcalde*—stmts adm, "I intend to go to the movies w/Frank."
>
> Letwin thinks *Alcalde* is inconsistent w/CEC 1250.

Statements for Purpose of Medical Diagnosis

BAJI—Statements to a doctor can be considered to show the basis of the doctor's opinion, but not for their truth.

> State-of-mind can be considered for truth.

FRE 803 (4)—broader than CEC—Statements can be considered for their truth, including stmts re the cause of injuries.

Limit of "for purposes of medical diagnosis or treatment"

> Arguably if reason for exam is litigation—stmts don't qualify.

CEC 1252—Stmts can be excluded if circumstances indicate lack of trustworthiness.

> Burden under this § would be on opponent.
>
> Determined under CEC 405 by the Ct.

Business Record

FRE 803 (6)

Reliability based on independent incentive to be accurate & internal controls.

"Business" defined very loosely—self-employed, part-time can still be a "business."

FF—kept in course of regularly conducted business activity

>Regular practice to make the record.

>All may be shown by custodian of records.

Too hard to prove up FF for recorded recollection.

Implicit reqmt that keeping the record relate to the regular course of the business.

>Keeping witness statements (RR) as part of business—outside *Palmer v. Hoffman*

Be careful of multiple hearsay in business record.

Some discretion about what is w/in the scope of the business—what can legitimately be in the record.

>Ex: bullet caliber in hospital record

Prior Testimony

FRE 804 (b)(1)—unavail req'd

FF—Usually introduced thru use of transcript.

>Transcript itself is hearsay.

>>Business record 803 (6)

>>Official record 803 (8)

>>Recorded recollection 803 (5) would have to bring reporter in to testify.

Adverse party, or predecessor in interest must have had opportunity and motive to cross-ex at prior hearing. Doesn't matter if actually cross-ex.

>Predecessor in interest only in civil trials & strictly construed.

CEC 1292—Permits prior testimony to be admitted against a present party who was not a party to the prior action so long as opportunity and similar motive to cross-ex.

CEC 1291—As against a party to prior action.

>If they offered it before, comes in.

>If offered vs them before, comes in if party at prior action had opportunity & motive to cross-ex.

CEC also has unavail reqmt.

>Cuts off objections to form not made below (1291) & objections based on competency or privilege not existing below (1291 & 1292).

FRE (incorporating FRCP by implicit reference) would waive objections not made below if they could have been made and cured—"formal" objections.

Note that CEC does not cover depos taken in same action; governed by CCP (same as FRCP).

Underlying objections to hearsay:

>Lack of foundation

>Lack of personal knowledge

>Impermissible opinion—borderline b/w substance & form

>>Usually considered formal

Prior Statements of Witness

FRE 801 (d)(1)(A)

>Classified as nonhearsay—adm for its truth.

>Witness must be avail for cross-ex presently.

>Prior statement made under oath.

>Inconsistent w/present testimony.

>>Cal. *Green* doctrine—inconsistent in effect

CEC 1235—Adm if witness' present testimony is inconsistent.

>Declarant avail for cross-ex & demeanor.

>Hearsay statement closer in time to the events.

>Concerns about turncoat witness.

>*Ulis* case—phone call; "I don't remember"; denial of contents of phone call; hearing testimony to jury; phone call evid

>Statement III may have come in as inconsistent w/statement II re present recollection.

Contrast w/Declaration vs Interest:

>Unavail req'd

>FRE 804 (a)(3)—testifying to lack of memory = unavail

>CEC 240—doesn't include lack of memory w/in "unavail"

>>If witness refuses to testify for fear of safety—"mental infirmity" w/in CEC 240 (a)(3).

>>*People v. Rojas*

If statement can't come in under prior inconsistent stmt, prior testimony, or declaration vs interest—it might make it for impeachment under FRE 806.

>If adm under FRE 806, no need for witness to have opp to explain as under FRE 613.

Prior consistent stmt FRE 801 (d)(1)(B)

>Only to rebut express or implied charge of recent fabrication or improper motive.

Unavailability

Determined as FF under FRE 104 (a) & CEC 405 by the Ct.

>May still offer evid as going to weight and credibility.

CEC 240 is broader than FRE

Witness not subject to the court's process (out-of-state)

Witness absent despite proponent's reasonable obligence

Privileged

Disqualified

Dead or unable to testify b/c of mental or physical infirmity

FRE 804 (a)

Privileged

Refuses to testify

Lack of memory

Dead or physical/mental infirmity

Absent & proponent unable to procure attendance or testimony by process—implies should use discovery devices like depos before hearsay comes in.

Confrontational Const Right & Unavail

Barber v. Page—prisoner in fed pen not const unavail

Mancusi v. Stubbs—out of country is const unavail

No need to try to persuade witness to return.

Ohio v. Roberts—Issuing supoenas to witness' home is good enough if whereabouts unknown.

Proving Unavail

Out of court stmts to prosecution establishing unavail might come in not for their truth, but to establish the prosecution's reasonable diligence.

Other Exceptions

Judgments FRE 803 (22)

Must be felony conviction.

Guilty plea—adm as admission, not really w/in judgments exception

Convictions of others only adm for impeachment.

Convictions of acc adm to prove essential facts.

Hearsay & Const

Green USSCt said so long as declarant avail for cross-ex either when stmt made or at trial the confrontation clause is complied w/.

Dutton v. Evans co-consp stmt to cell mate implicating Evans.

Ohio v. Roberts (1980)

In usual case, prosecution must produce or demonstrate the unavail of the hearsay declarant.

Exception where utility of trial confrontation very remote.

Once unavail shown, hearsay must be possessed of indicia of reliability.

Reliability can be inferred if w/in firmly rooted exception.

Otherwise need particularized guarantees of trustworthiness.

Codefendants

Admission of Δ is adm vs B as declaration vs interest if Δ is unavail at trial—takes the 5th. Issue if stmt makes it as "vs interest" b/c of self-serving qualities.

Bruton if joint trial admitting evid vs Δ & giving limiting instruction as to B isn't good enough (assuming evid inadm vs B).

Nelson v. O'Neil—Δ took stand in joint trial & repudiated prior confession.

Const adm in joint trial w/limiting instruction given as to B b/c B has opp to cross-ex Δ on stmt.

Lot easier to go w/separate trials or separate juries.

Const Right to Admt Evid

Chambers v. Miss—Δ offered confession of M, another person to the charged crime, M repudiated confession at trial, not allowed to impeach or offer stmts as declarations vs interest.

Under facts & circumstances here—viol of D/P

McMartin case—closed circuit TV testimony:

Denies right to cross-ex in open court.

Lose many subtle demeanor factors re credibility.

Prejudice to Δ: implication of need to protect

Critique of Hearsay

Making general rule like for relevance would just force Cts to create the rules all over again.

People v. Castro on Prop 8 § 28. Convictions admitted w/o limitation—still subject to CEC 352. So although rigid Ct created guidelines overruled, Ct will create anew under 352.

Abolished *Spearman* rule re prior convictions (dishonesty) in favor of "moral turpitude" including poss of heroin for sale but not poss of heroin.

Dallas County creating new exceptions:

Easier to get a Ct to stretch an existing exception.

Privileges

Not in FRE

Rationales

Protecting certain relationship of value to society

Guarding against invasion of privacy

Professional integrity

CEC 911—Cts have no power to expand on statutory priv.

Attorney-Client CEC 950–962

Common law priv as opposed to const priv

CEC 954—priv to prevent disclosure of conf comm between A&C

Definitions:

> CEC 950—"Lawyer" must be reasonably believed to be auth to practice law.
>
> CEC 951—"Client"—person or auth rep who consults lawyer for purpose of retaining L or securing legal service or advice.
>
> CEC 952—"Conf comm"—info transmitted in course of A-C relationship in conf.
>
> CEC 917—Creates a presumption of conf.

Joint holders CEC 952 contemplates presence of 3d parties to further C's interests or to whom disclosure is necessary

> CEC 912 (b) one joint holder cannot waive the other's priv as to what L said, what nonwaiving holder said, and what waiving holder said to the extent it reveals what nonwaiving holder said.
>
> Distinction b/w protecting the comm & the underlying facts

Waiver

> CEC 912 (a)—voluntary disclosure to 3d party is waiver
>
> Only the client can waive—unauth disclosures by others do not constitute waiver.
>
> > Circumstances (prior disclosures of the info) may indicate comm not intended to be conf.

Crime or fraud exception—CEC 956

> No priv if services of L sought to aid or plan crime.
>
> Depends on how comm characterized.

Proving FF: Can't disclose comm in ruling on priv.

> For crime/fraud exception might be able to ask L "did C say X" if clear that saying X would bring comm within exception.

Identity of client is not usually considered priv.

> The existence of the relationship is a FF for the priv.
>
> Dispute exists as to priv re anonymous payments to the IRS.

A communication may be:

> (1) assertive verbal conduct.
>
> (2) unintended transmission of info (C's appearance).
>
> (3) nonassertive but intended transmission of info (fingerprints, exam by doctor).

Info disclosed even to agents of A (doctor) may still be priv—*City & County of San Fran.*

Corporations & the A-C priv:

> *Upjohn* case—USSCA rejected limiting A-C priv to the "Control Group" of a Corp.
>
> > Protecting need for free flow of info w/in corp.

Creates the danger of veil of secrecy:

Ability of corp to immunize comm by making def cnsl party to them.

Tangible physical evid:

Olwell—Def Cnsl must, after a reasonable time, turn physical evid over to the prosecution but need not reveal the source.

Prosecution could not compel Δ himself to turn over the knife by subpoena.

Meredith—If Def Cnsl, or his agent, finds & removes physical evid, the location or source is adm b/c Def Cnsl has prevented prosecution from finding.

If the Δ still has evid, L may give advice as to legal consequences but may not cnsl client to commit a crime.

MRCP—lawyer may but need not disclose if necessary to prevent death or serious bodily harm.

CEC 956 doesn't apply—not compelled testimony in a hearing.

Interspousal Priv

CEC 970—Married person has priv not to testify against spouse.

Rather liberal interpretation of scope of "testify against."

CEC 971—Married person has priv not to be called at all by party adverse to spouse if spouse is a party to the action.

CEC 980—Married person has priv to prevent disclosure of conf comm b/w self & spouse during the marriage—priv exists after marriage.

Questions of what is intended as a communication.

Designed to encourage free flow of info b/w spouses.

Salazar—Const aspect:

X confessed to wife about murder, wife told police.

Not a waiver as to X—joint holder of priv.

X can prevent wife (or anybody else) from disclosing.

Alaska SCt said unconst—viol of confrontation clause.

Const priv vs public policy priv

Testimony was crucial.

Possibility of finding const basis for interspousal priv from *Giswold* penumbra.

The importance of the relationship

If state is asserting priv, refusing to disclose while prosecuting, might be unfair.

Psychiatric Priv

Lifschutz Cal SCt

Patient has priv to prevent disclosure—a qualified priv.

Exception if patient tenders his mental/emotional cond as an issue.

Doesn't put entire history avail for disclosure.

Professional Publications, Inc. • Belmont, CA

Burden on patient to show that a given comm is not directly related to the issue he tendered.

CEC 1016—patient litigant exception

Patient dangerous exception CEC 1024:

No priv if psych reasonably believes patient dangerous & disclosure necessary to prevent danger.

Tarasoff—imposed duty on psych to potential victims of patient—duty to warn

Establishing FF for exception:

CEC 915—prevents disclosure of comm to determine existence of the privilege.

Might ask "Did patient ever say X?" if X prima facie evid of reasonable belief of dangerousness.

CEC 1010—Psych means:

(a) Person reasonably believed by patient to be auth to practice.

(b)–(e) Person actually licensed as psychologist; social worker; school psychologist; marriage, family, & child counselor.

CEC 1011—Patient means person who consults or submits to exam for diagnosis or treatment.

CEC 1012—3d persons can be present if to further patient's interests or necessary for accomplishment of purpose of consult.

Official Info & ID of Informer

CEC 1040—priv for official info

CEC 1041—priv for public entity to refuse to disclose informant ID

CEC 1042—requires compensatory orders vs the govt if the priv is asserted to prevent disclosure in a criminal prosecution

As the interest of justice requires, leaves the content of the order entirely in the court's discretion.

Official info is info acquired by a public employee & not previously disclosed to the public.

The public entity & not the source of the info is the holder of the priv.

Here disclosure must be made to the public & by one authorized to do so—to waive.

Even if Ct determines that disclosure of the info if not against the public interest (CEC 1040 (b)(2)), prosecutor may have discretion to refuse.

Informer ID

CEC 1042 (c)—Unless informer is material witness on issue of guilt or innocence, info provided by him is adm w/o revealing his ID if court satisfied the info came from a reliable informant.

CEC 1042 (b)—Prosecution not req'd to reveal informer ID to litigate P/C issue on search warrant.

Tough case when affidavit reveals informer is a material witness but the prosecution doesn't intend to call him.

Sanction if no disclosure:

Rule in favor of party seeking disclosure on the issue.

Dismiss the case.

Hold the prosecutor in contempt.

News Reporter Priv

Bransburg USSCA—No 1st Am right to refuse to disclose source to grand jury.

Farber—No absolute priv but priv will be upheld if inquirer can't show a compelling need.

Material & relevant evid for criminal defense otherwise unavail is a compelling need.

Δ's 6th Am rights triumph over statutory priv.

Nixon (executive priv) similarly qualified priv—yielded to demands of criminal justice system.

In *Farber*—burden on inquirer to make threshold showing before getting to in-camera inspection for determination by the judge of relevance, materiality, & overbreadth.

Cal Shield Law—in Cal Const:

Can't hold reporter in contempt for refusal to disclose.

No other sanction avail.

Parent-Child Priv

People v. Doe—NY Ct found const underpinnings but left to state legis to create priv.

Ct contemplated priv waivable by parents.

Priest-Penitent Priv

Absolute priv—no exceptions

Both parties hold the priv—CEC 1033 & 1031.

Penitential communication = in conf; in presence of no 3d person so far as penitent is aware; to clergyman auth to hear & under duty to keep secret CEC 1032.

If penitent is dead, incompetent, or fails to claim, the priest can claim or waive the priv.

Authentication

Proving that the proffered evid is indeed what the proponent claims it to be; that a writing is genuine.

FRE 901 (a)—Authentication as a condition for adm is satisfied by evid suff to support a finding (prima facie).

FRE 901 (b)—Illustrations

(4) distinctive characteristics—contents disclose info w/in peculiar knowledge of purported originator

(3) comparison w/exemplar

Genuineness of exemplar

FRE 104 (b)—prima facie

CEC 1417—to satisfaction of court

Qualification of expert

FRE 104 (a)—to satisfaction of court

CEC 405

(5) voice identification

(6) telephone conversation—evid that ph # assigned to the person or business

(A) For person, self-ID or other circumstances

(B) For business, that conversation related to business

Direct auth:

Subscribing witness

Witness to act of signing

Best Evidence Rule

Really document original rule FRE 1002

Issues:

What is a "writing"—car license plate?

What constitutes an effort to prove the content of the writing?

Is the matter at issue collateral FRE 1004 (4)?

What is an original?

FRE 1001 (3)—A negative or any print therefrom is an "original" picture.

FRE 1001 (4)—Xerox copies are "duplicates"—adm as originals unless:

(1) genuine issue as to authenticity of original.

(2) unfair to admit the duplicate.

Simultaneous oral confession & tape recording:

Does oral testimony have independent existence, or is it more like reading a document as someone signs it?

Exceptions—originals not needed FRE 1004:

(1) Original lost or destroyed, unless in bad faith.

(2) Original in possession of opponent.

CEC has hierarchical rule: original-copies-oral testimony.

FRE—If original not necessary then copies & oral testimony equally admissible.

Ex of reporter's transcript of Δ's testimony:

Hearsay level one—Δ's stmt adm as an admission

Hearsay level two—reporter's stmt adm as business record or as public record

Authenticating the transcript:

The certificate itself isn't good enough—it is hearsay itself but arguably part of the record.

If business record, need the testimony of the custodian.

If public record FRE 901 (b)(7)—evidence that transcript is from clerk of court's office is good enough.

Experts

Experts allowed to give opinion in response to hypothetical question.

Experts may also simply state opinion & force the other side to bring out underlying assumptions.

FRE 705 allows but does not require hypothetical questions.

Hypos req'd at common law

Barefoot v. Texas—USSCt Texas death penalty case

Hypo may include controverted facts.

Should be suff evid to support finding each fact.

Δ can pose alternate hypo using his version of facts.

Not necessary that psych examine Δ.

No ultimate issue objection FRE 704.

Proper subject for expert:

Scientific, technical, or specialized knowledge that will assist trier of fact FRE 702

Sufficiently beyond common experience CEC 801

What expert may consider:

Facts in evid

Statements made for purposes of diagnosis FRE 803 (4)

Facts or data perceived by him at or before the hearing

FRE 703 (adm for truth)

Data of a type reasonably relied on by the profession even if not admissible FRE 703

This data may be disclosed on cross-ex FRE 705 but not considered for truth by the jury.

Frye controversy:

Special reliability standard—generally accepted in the scientific commonly for new scientific principles/process.

Maine court rejected *Frye* test for voiceprints *Williams*.

Cal court adopted *Frye* test for voiceprints *Kelley.*

Expert himself can't establish general acceptance.

Must consult scientific literature

Not hearsay—considered to show dispute or lack thereof

Learned treatise exception

If under FRE 104 (a)—no problem

Usually an expert can lay the foundation for adm of scientific evid, like lay witness providing personal knowledge FF.

Shirley—hypnosis:

The testimony of a witness who has undergone hypnosis is inadm unless *Frye* standard is met.

Dangers:

    Confabulation

    Difficulty of evaluating

    Inability to cross-ex

Hypnosis witness is now "unavail" for purposes or using prior testimony.

Course Mini-Outline

This is a sample of a mini-outline, which we recommend you create while studying for final exams to reinforce the course material and assist you in studying. This example was created from the evidence outline contained in the previous appendix.

Again, the use of abbreviations and sentence fragments should be governed by what works best for you. You should be able to reduce four to eight pages of your full course outline to one page of your mini-outline. The formality of the structure should also be tailored to your personal predilections. The organization may change somewhat from that in your full course outline as your understanding of the course material crystallizes. Your goal is to have a document that you can quickly scan to review the course material, with certain phrases or headings triggering a host of related rules and information.

Evidence Mini-Outline

Relevance 401 & 402

Immateriality—fact itself doesn't matter

Irrelevance—evid doesn't tend to prove fact

Balancing 403—admitted unless probity subst outweighed by prejudice

Issue must be in dispute for evidence to be relevant.

FRE 407—subseq corrective measures not adm to show negl

FRE 103—reversible error

Burden of proof for relevance on the proponent

Opinion

FRE 602—Personal knowledge req't

Prima facie standard as FF—may be provided by the witness

FRE 701—Lay witness opinion

(1) rationally based on perception

(2) helpful to understanding witness' testimony

FRE 704—ultimate issue not objectionable

Formal Objections

FRE 611—Leading questions

Allowed on cross-ex. Permitted on direct of adv party or witness identified w/ adv party.

Ct has discretion to control examination.

FRE 611 (b)—Beyond the scope:

Cross-ex limited to subj matter of direct & credibility matters.

Ct has discretion to permit beyond the scope.

Character Evid

FRE 404—Char evid inadm to prove conforming conduct.

> Acc may offer pertinent traits of himself or victim.

> Once acc offers evid; prosecution may offer evid in rebuttal.

> Pros may offer evid of homicide victim's peacefulness to rebut evid of initial aggressor.

FRE 405—Methods

> Opinion or reputation permissible forms:

>> Specific acts can be inquired into on cross-ex.

> Specific acts adm if char is essential element.

FRE 404 (b)—Other wrongs:

> Not adm to show conforming conduct.

> Adm to show intent, motive, common scheme, or plan.

> Prima facie standard for FF that acc committed other wrongs.

FRE 608—Character of testifying witness for truthfulness

> Opinion & rep permissible forms

> Specific acts may be inquired into on cross-ex:

>> As to testifying witness' credibility

>> As to witness about whom credibility witness testified

> No extrinsic evid of specific acts.

> Evid of truthful char adm only after witness' char attacked.

FRE 609—Prior convictions

> crime punishable by one year or

> crime involving dishonesty or false stmt

> Method: can elicit from witness on cross-ex or establish by public record

> Subject to balancing similar to FRE 403 except tilted in favor of exclusion.

>> Might have to prove to Ct witness actually convicted before inquiry permitted.

FRE 406—Habit adm to prove conforming conduct.

Prior Inconsistent Statements Going to Credibility

FRE 613 (a)—Witness need not be shown or receive disclosure of the contents of the statement prior to inquiry.

> (b)—Statement inadm unless witness has opportunity to explain.

FRE 610—Can't impeach with religious beliefs.

Collateral impeachment

> By analogy to FRE 608, may permit inquiry on cross-ex but no extrinsic evid.

Rape Evid

FRE 412—Opinion and rep re V's past sexual behavior inadm.

Specific acts of V adm:

(1) If const req'd

(2) To show Δ not the source of the semen/injury

(3) Past conduct w/acc

Screening procedure before evid goes to jury.

Hearsay

FRE 801—statement other than by witness on the stand offered to prove the truth of the matter asserted therein.

Burden on the opponent to show assertiveness of stmt/conduct.

Statement must be offered for its truth.

Legally operative language

Statements that reveal info about the declarant

Statements that have effect on the hearer

Decl v. Interest FRE 804 (B)(5)

Unavailability req'd

Vs interest at time statement made

Pecuniary or proprietary interest or civil or criminal liability

Most Cts do not sever partly self-serving & vs interest statements.

Vs interest may depend on offeror's purpose.

Admissions FRE 801 (d)(2)

Inculpatory/exculpatory character doesn't matter.

Personal knowledge not necessary

(A) by the party.

(B) adopted by the party.

(C) by one authorized to speak for the party.

(D) by an agent relating to matters w/in scope of agency.

Coconspirator FRE 801 (d)(2)(E)

FF—that a conspiracy existed & declarant in consp w/acc

Determined by judge alone—more than prima facie standard.

In furtherance requirement—not strictly construed.

Temporal limits—traditionally ended at arrest.

Alt—includes concealment phase.

Past Recollection Recorded FRE 803 (5)

Writing made or adopted by witness when fresh in memory & reflects matter accurately.

Can have multiparty proof.

Witness must have present inability to recollect.

Writing read, not admitted into evid.

> May be offered by opponent.

Past Recollection Refreshed

Unless offered in evid, writing used to refresh is not objectionable as hearsay.

Genuineness of witness' recollection is FF under prima facie standard.

Opponent may offer the writing.

Writings used to refresh are discoverable FRE 612.

Prior Identification FRE 801 (d)(1)(c)

Declarant must testify at trial & be subject to cross-ex.

Present Sense Impression FRE 803 (1)

Contemporaneous event perceived by the declarant.

FF can be shown by circumstances & contents of stmt (under 104 (a)—satisfaction of Ct).

Excited Utterance FRE 803 (2)

Statement relating to startling event while declarant under stress of excitement.

Dying Decl FRE 804 (b)(2)

Under belief of impending death.

> Related to cause or circumstances of death only.

FF can be established by stmt itself.

> Under FRE 104 (a)—Ct's satisfaction

State of Mind FRE 803 (3)

State of mind in issue, or

Intent to prove later conduct in accordance therewith. Problem when mixed w/intents of others.

Exception for stmt of belief or memory to prove facts remembered or believed.

For Purpose of Medical Diagnosis FRE 803 (4)

Must be for purpose of medical treatment or diagnosis.

Includes statements about causes of injuries.

Business Record FRE 803 (6)

Kept in course of regular business activity.

Regular practice to make the record, & must relate to business.

"Business" defined loosely.

Potential for multiple hearsay.

Prior Testimony FRE 801 (b)(1)

Adv party must have had opportunity & similar motive to cross-ex at prior hearing.

For civil cases, adv party may have been pred-in-interest.

Incorporating FRCP would waive objections not made below if they could have been cured upon objection—formal obj.

Opinion is considered formal.

Prior Statements—Inconsistent FRE 804 (d)(1)(A)

Witness avail for cross-ex—present testimony, inconsistent.

Prior statement made under oath.

Possible inconsistent in effect for "I don't remember."

If no oath & witness avail, might still use for impeachment under FRE 806.

Prior Consistent Statement FRE 804 (d)(1)(B)

Only to rebut charge of fabrication, bias, etc.

Judgments FRE 803 (22)

Felony convictions—vs acc only to show elements of offenses

Foundational Facts FRE 104 (a) & (b)

(a) Ct determines—to Ct's satisfaction—final determination.

May consider inadm evid except evid barred by priv.

Can hold hearing in jury's presence (discretionary).

Except voluntariness issue for confessions.

As to qual of witness, existence of priv, admissibility of evid.

(b) Ct makes prima facie determination—sufficient to support a finding—jury makes final decision.

May not consider inadm evid

As to relevance of evid depending on existence of fact

(e) Evid relevant to weight and credibility comes in.

Unavailability

Determined as FF under 104 (a) to Ct's satisfaction.

Privileged

Refuses to testify

Lack of memory

Dead or physical/mental illness/infirmity

Absent or unable to procure attendance or testimony by process—reasonable diligence

Const reqmt

Prisoner in state pen not good enough; out of country is OK; whereabouts unknown & subpoenas sent to last address OK.

Hearsay & Const Confront Clause

Prosecution must produce declarant or demonstrate unavail.

Except where utility of trial confront minimal

Once unavail shown—hearsay must have indicia of reliability.

Firmly rooted hearsay exception

Otherwise need particular guarantees of trustworthiness

Codef & Confront Clause

When Δ's confession adm in joint trial & implicates B (assuming inadm vs B).

If Δ takes 5th—limiting instruction not good enough.

If Δ takes the stand & B has opp to cross-ex—OK.

Const Right to Admt Evid

D/P problem

Privileges

Attorney Client CEC 950–962

Lawyer—reasonably believed auth to practice law by client

Client—consults for purpose of retaining or getting advice.

Conf comm—info transmitted (both ways) in conf in course of relationship.

3d parties present to further client's interest or to whom disclosure is necessary is not waiver.

Client is priv holder—can prevent others from disclosing.

Joint holders cannot waive the other's priv.

Waiver—only client can waive.

Crime or fraud exception

Comm can't be disclosed to rule on priv.

Corporate priv extends further than just to control group.

Tangible Physical Evid

Must turn over after reasonable time.

If removed by lawyer or agent, location is disclosed & adm.

Interspousal Priv

Both spouses hold priv.

Priv to not testify against spouse (spouse need not be party).

Priv not to be called as witness by adv party if spouse is party.

Priv to prevent disclosure of conf comm made during the marriage.

Const aspect—yields to acc's confront rights.

Psych-Patient Priv

Psych means—reasonably believed by patient to be psych or actually licensed psychologist, SW, school psych, MFC.

Patient—consults or submits to exam for diagnosis and treatment.

Patient is priv holder.

Patient—litigant exception:

Patient has burden to show given comm not related to issues he tendered.

Dangerous patient exception—reasonable belief patient dangerous and disclosure necessary.

Duty to warn—*Tarasoff*

3d persons can be present to conf comm w/o losing priv.

Official Info

Info acquired in conf by public employee and not disclosed to public.

Public entity is priv holder.

Not disclosed if against public interest.

Compensatory order req'd in criminal case if no disclosure.

Informer ID

Not req'd to reveal ID to litigate P/C on search warrant.

Unless material witness on guilt or innocence issue, info is adm w/o revealing ID.

Ct must be satisfied reliable informant (FRE 104 (a)).

Compensatory order req'd here only if nondisclosure would deprive acc of a fair trial.

Newsman Priv

Cal Shield—can't hold newsman in contempt for refusal to disclose.

Priv not absolute.

Inquirer must show compelling need—material and relevant and otherwise unavail for criminal def—to make the threshold showing to get in camera hearing for relevance, materiality, and overbreadth.

Parent-Child

Waiting for legis

Conceived as waivable by parents.

Priest-Penitent

Absolute priv

Both parties are holders.

No 3d parties present.

Authentication FRE 901 (a)

FF of authenticity determined under prima facie test.

Distinctive characteristics

Comparison w/exemplar

FF—genuineness of exemplar—prima facie; expert qualification—Ct's satisfaction

Voice ID

Telephone conversation

Self-authentication FRE 902

Direct auth

Best Evid Rule FRE 1002

Must use original doc to prove its contents.

What is a writing—is it offered to prove its contents?

Photos—prints or the negative are originals.

Xerox copies—"duplicates" adm as originals unless:

(1) Genuine issue as to auth of original

(2) Unfair to use

Exceptions:

(1) Original lost or destroyed

(2) Original in possession of opponent

(3) Collateral matters

Experts FRE 702

Testify by hypo or direct opinion.

Proper subject for expert—special knowledge of assistance to trier.

Expert may consider:

Facts in evid

Statement made for purpose of diagnosis

Facts perceived by him

Data of a type reasonably relied on by the profession—even if inadm
    May be disclosed on cross-ex FRE 705
    Not adm for truth
Frye standard
    Special reliability—new scientific process generally accepted

Professional Publications, Inc. ▪ Belmont, CA

Class Flowchart

Besides a regular outline and a mini-outline, you may also want to prepare flowcharts for your classes. Like mini-outlines, flowcharts should be used to help trigger key legal concepts and issues while studying for midterms or finals. Accordingly, they should also be kept to a minimal length. This appendix consists of a sample flowchart covering certain tort issues and concepts.*

Δ	defendant	R & D	research and development
π	plaintiff	SL	strict liability
A/R	assumption of risk	T	time
CN	contributory negligence	w/in	within
N	negligence	w/o	without

Strict Liability in Tort

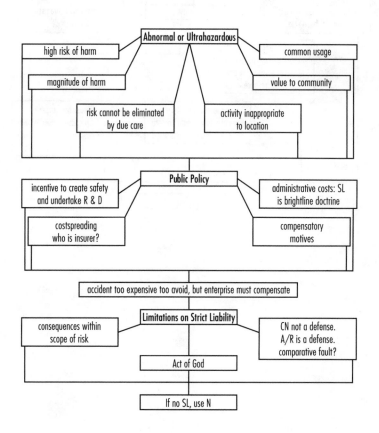

Products Liability

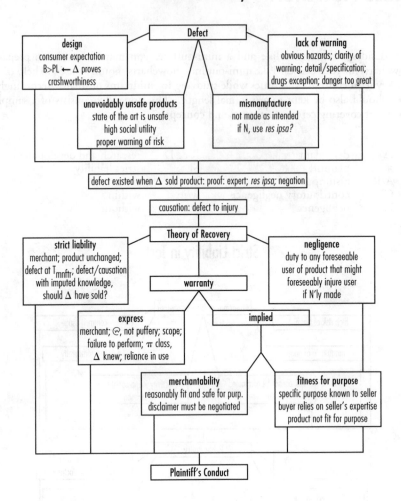

Defamation

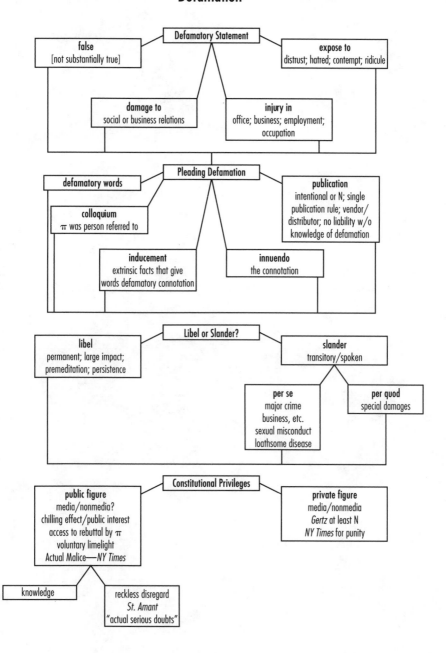

*Rachel Krevans, Esq. (University of California, Davis Law School, Class of 1984), prepared this flowchart. The authors gratefully acknowledge her contribution.

Sample Exams

This part of the appendix contains two sample law school exams. The first exam covers matters that are typically discussed in first-year contract classes. The second is a sample property law test.

We recommend that you take these sample exams under formal test conditions at the midpoint of your contract and property law courses. After you have finished your answers, compare them to the sample answers provided and read the comments that follow each answer.

Do not be overly concerned if your answers are not comparable to the sample answers provided. Your professors may not have covered some of the issues raised by the sample exams. Further, the sample answers have been edited and are thus probably more polished and comprehensive than those typically provided by law students (who generally do not have the time to edit their exam answers). Pay particular attention to the structure of the sample answers and the points made in the comment sections. If you missed issues, go back and reread the sample exam questions and underline the key words that raised the issues you overlooked. This technique will help you avoid missing similar issues in the future.

Sample Contracts Exam

Contract exam questions usually focus primarily on formation issues (i.e., was an enforceable contract formed) or alternatively, on issues of performance and remedies for nonperformance (i.e., was the contract breached and, if so, what are the parties rights). This sample question is typical of the first type of contract exam questions.

Sample Question

Mr. A, a rancher, owned 40 acres of largely open land. For many years, Ms. B, who lived next door, had let her sheep roam and graze freely on Mr. A's land. In July of this year, Mr. A decided to build a house on the 40 acres. Before he started construction, he notified Ms. B by letter on July 15 that she had no right to let her sheep use his land for a pasture. He stated in the letter, however, that the sheep could continue to use his land if Ms. B paid him $200 a month (the local standard rate for renting pasture land).

After Ms. B received Mr. A's letter, she met with him on July 28. During the meeting, she told him that she considered a reasonable rental rate for the land to be no more than $100 a month because a significant portion of the land was rocky. She also stated, however, that "I'll probably pay you (Mr. A) $200 a month for the use of the land if you really insist." During this meeting, Mr. A mainly talked about how much fun he was having building his house. Before Ms. B left, however, Mr. A told her that he would consider what she had said.

In August of this year, Ms. B continued to let her sheep use Mr. A's land without paying him anything. Mr. A was not happy. He had not yet received any money for this use of the land, but he did not say anything to Ms. B about his displeasure because he was too busy working on his house. On September 1, Ms. B put a check for $100 in Mr. A's mailbox with a note that stated:

Mr. A, here is a check for the use of your land by my sheep for September. I will send you a check for October near the end of this month.

After Mr. A got the check for $100, he cashed it. The sheep used Mr. A's property without incident for the next three weeks. On September 24, Ms. B put another check for $100 in Mr. A's mailbox. After he got the check, Mr. A immediately sent the following letter to Ms. B (dated September 25):

Dear Ms. B:

Enclosed please find your check for $100. I never agreed to let you and your sheep use my land for anything less than $200 a month. You and your sheep kept using my land for the last two months after I told you this. Accordingly, you owe me $200 for the use of the land for the month of August. You also owe me another $100 for September. If you want your sheep to use my land for this month, or any other month, it will cost you $200 per month as we agreed.

Sincerely, Mr. A

After Ms. B received the preceding letter she became quite upset, feeling that he had reneged on their "deal." Nonetheless, she managed to walk over to Mr. A's newly built house. She then calmly informed him that, as far as she was concerned, Mr. A had agreed to rent her the land for $100 a month for as long as she wanted it and that her sheep could keep using the land for years if she continued to pay. She also told him that she was going to give Mr. A $100 for the month of August, but that after receiving his letter, she had decided not to do so. She also told Mr. A that if he was not happy with their deal, he could sue. Mr. A told Ms. B that she would soon be hearing from his attorney.

Please discuss the rights and obligations of Mr. A and Ms. B, if any, with respect to this situation.

Exam Answer

I. Introduction

Mr. A's and Ms. B's rights and obligations depend largely on the application of the rules of law concerning how contracts are formed, particularly those concerning how an offer can be accepted, the statute of frauds, and quasi-contracts, explained as follows.

II. Mr. A's Original Offer

Generally, the formation of a contract requires an objective manifestation of mutual consent to a specific exchange supported by consideration. The manifestation of mutual assent to an exchange ordinarily takes the form of an offer or proposal by one party communicated to another, followed by the other party's acceptance of the offer or proposal. An offer is simply an expression of willingness or intent to enter into a bargain that allows the offeree to reasonably conclude that the power to create a contract has been conferred upon her. Here, there is little question that Mr. A's July 15 letter constitutes an offer to Ms. B to enter into a contract with him whereby she would rent his land for her sheep for the sum of $200 per month. Specifically, it is an expression of intent by Mr. A to enter into a bargain with Ms. B should she agree to the terms specified therein.

A. Acceptance of Mr. A's Original Offer: Did it Occur?

1. Form of Acceptance

Was Mr. A's original offer ever accepted by Ms. B? A person accepts an offer to enter into a contract when he or she voluntarily manifests his or her consent to the terms proposed by the offeror. Unless the offer expressly indicates otherwise, an offer can be accepted in any manner that is reasonable under the circumstances. Normally, this takes the form of a promise by offeree to perform the terms offered by the offeror or the offeree's actual performance either in whole or in part of the terms proposed. Here, Mr. A offered to let Ms. B use his land for her sheep if she paid him $200 a month. Mr. A's offer invites Ms. B's performance by her payment of $200 a month to him. Thus, one could argue that this was the only means by which Ms. B could accept his offer. However, in his offer, Mr. A did not prescribe an exclusive manner of acceptance. If an offeror merely suggests a permitted method of acceptance, other methods of acceptance are not precluded. Thus, Ms. B was probably free to accept Mr. A's offer either by a return promise or by her performance.

2. Arguments for Acceptance of Original Offer

Did Ms. B accept Mr. A's offer by a return promise of performance or otherwise? After Ms. B received Mr. A's letter, she told him that "she would probably pay him $200 a month for the use of the land if he really insisted." In this case, Mr. A is insisting that Ms. B pay him $200 a month. The fact that Ms. B also arguably made a counteroffer at the same time (i.e., $100 a month for the use of the land) did not terminate Mr. A's original offer because she made clear in her conversation that she did not wish this to occur. Alternatively, Mr. A can also argue that the preceding statement to Ms. B was simply an inquiry (as opposed to a counteroffer, which normally operates to reject and terminate the original offer unless otherwise indicated by its terms) since her statement was ambiguous. Thus, Mr. A can argue that Ms. B accepted his offer by the preceding words.

Further, after this conversation occurred, Ms. B continued to let her sheep use Mr. A's land. As indicated previously, subsequent conduct of a party to whom an offer has been made can serve as acceptance of the same. Here, Mr. A left no doubt that Ms. B and her sheep could not use his land unless they agreed to pay him $200 a month. Accordingly, even if the quoted statement did not serve to accept Mr. A's offer in and of itself, Mr. A can argue that it, in conjunction with Ms. B's subsequent use of the land, constituted an acceptance of his offer.

Finally, Ms. B's tender of a check to Mr. A for only $100 can viewed as just part performance for that month. It was apparently not specified on the check that it was intended to constitute payment in full for the rental of the property for September or otherwise. Also, Ms. B's letter stated that "a check" was enclosed for September, language that could lead Mr. A to reasonably conclude that the balance of the rent for that month would be forthcoming.

Under this analysis, and assuming that the "agreement" was sufficiently definite to be enforced as discussed as follows, Ms. B would owe Mr. A $200 for the use of the land in August and $100 for September (but see Section B *infra*). Ms. B would also have to pay Mr. A $200 a month if she wanted to keep using the land in the future for her sheep.

3. Arguments against Acceptance of Original Offer and Acceptance of Counteroffer

On the other hand, Ms. B can argue that she never accepted Mr. A's offer to rent the land for $200 a month either verbally or by her actions. Specifically, to be effective, an acceptance of an offer must be clear and unequivocal. Because she stated that she would "probably" accept Mr. A's offer to rent the land for $200 a month, her initial response to Mr. A's offer was not unequivocal.

Additionally, Ms. B can argue that she made a verbal counteroffer to rent the land for $100 a month during their meeting on July 26. This counteroffer was reconfirmed by her letter of September 1. No express method of acceptance was communicated with the counteroffer. After the end of their July 26 meeting, Mr. A also told Ms. B that he would consider her comments. Ms. B can thus argue that Mr. A accepted her counteroffer by cashing the $100 check. Mr. A apparently did not write anything on the check to indicate to the contrary. Prior to cashing the check, he also did not tell her either verbally or in writing that he was rejecting her counteroffer.

Ms. B can also argue that Mr. A is not entitled to any money from her for the use of the land for the month of August since she had not expressly accepted his offer to rent the land for $200 a month prior thereto. Moreover, her conduct in letting her sheep use the land should not be construed as part performance constituting acceptance of Mr. A's offer, since the performance sought by Mr. A's offer was the tender of $200, and not sheep roaming freely across his land. Ms. B may also be able to argue that she was entitled to use the land based on the acquisition of a prescriptive easement since the sheep had used his land for many years in the past apparently without Mr. A's permission. (Note, however, that even if one accepts the preceding analysis, Ms. B could still be liable to Mr. A for damages based on a quasi-contract theory as discussed *infra* for her sheep's use of the land in August.)

Under this analysis, Ms. B would not owe Mr. A any money presently. She would, however, be required to pay him at least $100 a month for any future use of the land assuming a sufficiently definite contract had been entered into as discussed in the next section. Also, if their agreement is construed as a month-to-month tenancy terminable upon 30-days notice to either party (see next section), Mr. A could force her to pay $200 a month rent to use the land by giving her 30-days notice canceling their current agreement. Mr. A's letter of September 25 might be interpreted as constituting such notice.

Ms. B may also want to argue that even if she agreed to rent the land from Mr. A for $200 a month, Mr. A waived his right to insist on the payment of such a sum for the month of September by cashing her rent check for $100. A waiver is the intentional relinquishment of a known right. Arguably, the cashing of a rent check for an amount less than that agreed upon without any notice to indicate that the landlord still intends to seek reimbursement for additional sums constitutes a waiver of any right to do so.

III. Requirement of Definiteness

For a contract to exist, the law requires that the agreement be sufficiently definite to enforce. In this case, either party could argue that no agreement was entered into between them because neither party made an offer that clearly spelled out the material terms of the contract, i.e., "How long can or must Ms. B keep using the land for her sheep—six months, a year? What was the amount of land rented? All 40 acres, including the curtilage of Mr. A's house, or some lesser area?"

However, even if terms of an agreement are not clearly spelled out, a court can sometimes interpret the agreement to include the missing term or terms from references to, among other things, standard and customary terms or practices. Other times, missing terms can be implied by law. In most jurisdictions, an agreement to rent land for a specified sum per month, but without any specified term, will be deemed by law to be an agreement for a month-to-month tenancy that is automatically renewed each month unless one of the parties to the agreement gives the other 30-days notice canceling the same. Also, such agreements are customarily treated in such a fashion by those who enter into them.

In sum, while an argument exists that any agreement entered into by the parties is too indefinite to enforce, a court would more than likely hold here that custom, practice, and the past dealings of the parties could fill the missing gaps.

IV. Statute of Frauds

Ms. B told Mr. A that they had a deal whereby she could rent the land for years for $100 a month. Assuming such an agreement exists, it might seem to be barred by the Statute of Frauds. Among other things, the Statute of Frauds bars the enforceability of agreements not to be performed within one year from the making thereof unless there is some written memorandum of the agreement signed by the party to be charged. Judicial hostility to the statute, however, has caused it to receive a narrow construction, such that only where it is impossible to perform the contract within one year is it unenforceable. Here, Ms. B's alleged lease for "as long as she wants" is not impossible to perform within one year, since she may no longer desire the land within that time.

Of course, if as suggested previously, their agreement (if one exists—see next section) is interpreted as creating a contract for the rental of Mr. A's property on a month-to-month basis, the contract would fall outside the Statute of Frauds, because it could be performed within a year since either party may cancel the same upon 30-days notice.

A court could also find that any agreement entered into between Mr. A and Ms. B based on the preceding facts falls outside the Statute of Frauds by finding that Mr. A's offer was divisible in that it called for a series of separate contract proposals for the rental of the land on a 30-day basis that Ms. B could accept or reject each month.

V. Arguments against the Formation of Any Contract

A. No Contract Arguments

Although it is certainly possible that a court would find that some type of contract was entered into by the parties as set forth previously, it is also conceivable that a court could find that no meeting of the minds occurred. More particularly, under the preceding facts, one could find that Ms. B never consented to Mr. A's offer, i.e., she neither expressly promised to pay Mr. A $200 a month nor tendered the sum to him. Moreover, one can argue that her conduct in letting her sheep continue to graze on Mr. A's property is not significant since she had been doing the same thing for many years.

Similarly, one could find that Mr. A never accepted her counteroffer in that he never expressly promised her that he would accept only $100 for her use of the land per month. He did, of course, accept her tender of this sum of money, but because the subject check did not specify payment in full one can objectively conclude that Mr. A did not intend to accept Ms. B's counteroffer by cashing it and he merely accepted it on account of the total rent due.

B. Quasi-Contractual Liability

If no contract was entered into between the parties, would Mr. A have any right to recover any sums from Ms. B? Even if no contract was entered into, Ms. B may be liable to Mr. A under a quasi-contract theory. Such contracts are not true contracts involving expressly bargained for consideration, but are implied by law and are usually based on the theory of unjust enrichment. Accordingly, the plaintiff must prove that the defendant received a benefit, and that the retention of the benefit without payment therefore would be unjust such as where the circumstances would indicate to a reasonable person that some payment for the benefit was expected.

A benefit gratuitously conferred cannot be used to find liability based on a quasi-contract theory since a person cannot reasonably expect to be paid for such a benefit. Here, there is no question that Ms. B received a benefit from being able to use Mr. A's land for her sheep. Further, the circumstances indicate that Mr. A did not gratuitously confer this benefit upon her. Rather, he expressly told her that he expected to be paid for such use. Ms. B might argue that Mr. A is not entitled to recover any sums from her under a quasi-contract theory for the month of August since he did not object to her use of the land during that month even though she did not pay him in advance for the use. However, this argument would probably fail, because Mr. A had already put her on notice that she would not be allowed to use his land for free. Moreover, the imposition of quasi-contract liability appears appropriate in this case since quasi-contract duties are often imposed where, as here, some direct relationship exists between the parties.

Under a quasi-contract theory, Mr. A would be entitled to recover from Ms. B a *quantum meruit* ("as much as he deserves") measure of damages. This would be the reasonable rental value of the property for use thereof whether it be $200 a month, $100 a month, or some other sum.

Mr. A may also possess tort remedies against Ms. B for her use of the land.

Answer Strategy

In taking contract exams, the student should first attempt to identify in broad terms what type of question she is being presented by the professor. Such an approach helps to identify the major issues presented by the question. However, the student should realize that many questions, while primarily focusing on either formation or performance issues, may cover some aspects of both.

Outline

Before beginning to write out any law school exam answer, a student should first identify the issues involved in the question. It is often helpful to create a short outline of your answer before analyzing the problem in more depth. The outline should briefly set forth the issues involved in the question. (See the sample Property Exam question for an alternative technique of annotating or marking up the exam question itself as a way of identifying the issues to be discussed in the answer.)

The purpose of the outline is to give you a road map for answering the subject question. It should be used to create the headings and subheadings for the answer and note issues. It should otherwise be kept very brief. You should generally not spend more than 10 to 15 minutes outlining a question for a 60-minute essay question since you will need the rest of the time to write an adequate essay answer. Outlining or issue-spotting and organization is important, but the majority of time spent responding to an essay exam question in law school should be devoted to actually writing an answer to the question. You should, however, try to specify in the outline or otherwise what key facts raised by the exam question relate to the main issues in the exam. Doing so will help you to apply the law to the specific facts set forth in the exam, an important quality that distinguishes good exam answers from bad ones.

Outlining a question is also useful if you find yourself in the unfortunate situation where you have misallocated your time and still have many issues to discuss and not enough minutes to do so. In that situation, you should outline your remaining exam answer in the test booklet being submitted to the professor to show that you have at least identified all of the issues involved in the question.

In such a situation, the detail presented in the outline will necessarily be dependant upon the time remaining to finish the question. For example, suppose that a student was presented with a three-hour essay exam with three different questions, including the question set forth previously. Also, suppose that the student decided to answer the question first and then spent 55 minutes on the question without addressing the statute of frauds or quasi-contract issues. The student should probably spend his remaining five minutes outlining these two issues and then move on to answer the other two questions. It would be a mistake for the student to fully write out answers to these two issues if, by doing so, he would cut into the time he would otherwise have had to answer the other two questions.

The following outline was used to answer the subject contracts question.

I. Introduction

Summarize main issues involved in question: formation issues; question of definiteness; statute of frauds; and quasi-contracts.

II. Mr. A's Original Offer

Mr. A's July 15 letter constitutes an offer.

A. Acceptance of Mr. A's Offer: Did it Occur?

    1. Form of Acceptance

Was Mr. A's original offer ever accepted by Ms. B? Possible acceptance either by performance or promise to perform. Mr. A did not prescribe an exclusive manner of acceptance.

    2. Arguments for Acceptance of Original Offer

Did Ms. B accept Mr. A's offer by a return promise of performance or otherwise?

Ms. B's statement "she would probably pay him $200 a month for the use of the land if he really insisted." Counteroffer/inquiry not terminate Mr. A's offer.

Use of land after offer construe as acceptance.

Tender of $100 check, construe as part performance re: not specified on the check that it constituted payment in full.

    3. Arguments against Acceptance of Original Offer and Acceptance of Counteroffer

No acceptance by Ms. B. Acceptance not unequivocal because of the word "probably."

Additionally, verbal counteroffer to rent the land for $100/July 26 meeting. Counteroffer reconfirmed by September 1 letter.

Accepted/cashing of $100 check by Mr. A. Not rejected by Mr. A before check cashed. Said consider her offer.

Ms. B's use of land not performance sought by Mr. A.

Waiver by Mr. A to insist on $200 a month/cashing check.

III. Requirement of Definiteness

Lease term is open-ended and not clearly spelled out, but terms can be implied by law.

IV. Statute of Frauds

Ms. B's statement use land for years/as long as I want. Take contract outside of statute/performance within a year possible/construe as month-to-month, offer series of contracts.

V. Arguments against the Formation of Any Contract

A. No agreement entered into between Mr. A and Ms. B.

B. Quasi-contract theory.

Discussion of Answer

The subject answer, while not representing the only possible organizational approach, does a good job of setting forth the applicable law and then applying it to the hypothetical fact pattern. Headings and subheadings were used judiciously. The author also wisely decided to only note that certain tort and property issues were raised by the exam question without discussing the same since such issues were obviously not covered by his contracts class. It is almost universally a mistake to discuss issues on an exam question where such issues were not discussed in class by your professor or covered in the assigned reading material.

On the negative side, however, the author probably spent too much time discussing what constitutes an offer in the abstract (see Section II). The author should have pithily described what constitutes an offer to enter into a contract in one sentence, instead of taking three long sentences to do so. The reason for this is that in a law school exam time is a precious commodity and should not be wasted on overly detailed discussions of general legal principles.

Sample Property Exam

Sample Question

S owned a three-story residential building in a seaside town; one unit was located on each floor. S lived in the upper unit, which he also used as the office for his yacht chartering business. In June 1990, S sold the building to B, an elderly widow. The sales agreement provided that S could "use the upper unit as his home and office for five years without payment of rent, since the purchase price was adjusted to compensate for this arrangement."

A small roof leak developed, resulting in persistent dripping in two areas in the upper unit, particularly during rainstorms. S was very familiar with such leaks, having fixed many of them in the building during the years, but made no effort to fix this one. As a sailor accustomed to waves and spray, he felt the drips were only a minor inconvenience. He did not mention the problem to B.

In November 1990, B leased the lower unit to T for 20 years for use as a residence. The written lease required a monthly rent of $1,000 and also stated:

> In addition to the monthly rent described above, Tenant shall pay the sum of $10,000 to Landlord as Bonus Rent when Tenant takes possession of the Premises. Such Bonus Rent shall be refunded to Tenant if the Premises are in good condition at the termination of this Lease. . . .

> Tenant may assign or sublease his interest provided that consent of Landlord is first obtained.

T paid the $10,000 and moved in.

In January 1991, X, a researcher studying termite behavior, applied to rent the vacant middle unit. B refused his application on the basis that she "didn't want to rent to a scientist." Later that month, T learned he was being transferred to Iowa, approached X, and worked out a tentative deal. T then asked for B's permission to assign or sublease to X. B refused consent. T ignored this and proceeded to enter into an agreement with X entitled "Sublease," which provided that X would occupy the lower unit for the balance of the lease term and pay the required rent to B, but that T would be entitled to the refund of bonus rent. X moved into the lower unit in February 1991. B subsequently accepted rental payments from X, though complaining each time that X had no rights in the unit.

On December 3, 1991, the whole building collapsed; a falling beam broke X's arm. An investigation revealed that three termites had accidentally escaped from one of X's jars and multiplied dramatically due to the unusual moisture conditions, and that millions of termites caused the collapse of the building.

Discuss the rights and liabilities of only the following:

(a) S and B (13 points)

(b) B and T (13 points)

(c) B and X (10 points)

(d) T and X (4 points)

Exam Answer

I. S and B

A. The Landlord-Tenant Relationship

The first issue raised is S's <u>possible</u> rights as a <u>tenant</u> or otherwise with respect to B. The sales agreement gave S the right to "use" the top unit as home and office for five years <u>without</u> paying rent. A problem is raised as to the <u>type of estate</u> S holds in the top unit. Typically, a leasehold estate is characterized by a <u>duty to pay rent</u> on the part of the tenant. Although the parties here have agreed no rent is to be paid for five years' use, the discount from the purchase price could essentially be viewed as five-years' rent reduced to present value and "paid" up front.

In this case, S has a <u>term of years tenancy</u> for five years. Since the sales agreement contains the names of the parties, the permitted uses, and (possibly) the "rent" term, it <u>may</u> sufficiently set forth the contract's material terms to satisfy the statute of frauds, which is applicable to leases for terms longer than one year. If not, the landlord's consent to the arrangement would probably save it from being void and render it a <u>tenancy-at-will</u>, terminable by either party.

Another possibility is that rather than a leasehold estate, S received a <u>license</u>— permission to use B's real property at B's will. Licenses are <u>not</u> subject to the statute of frauds, and are generally recoverable at the licensor's will. Here, however, the five-year term indicates there was no intent that S's right to use the top unit be revocable. Additionally, even if a license were created, it might be irrevocable because it is arguably <u>coupled with an interest</u> of S in the unit—the interest in his personal property consisting of furniture, business equipment, etc.

Another possibility is that S reserved an exclusive <u>easement</u> for five years in the top unit, for use as a home and office. The easement would be <u>in gross</u>, since it is <u>personal to S</u> and not tied to any parcel or piece of land. Since easements in gross are normally only granted for such simple and less involved uses as rights of way, utilities, and access, a court would probably be disinclined to find that S's rights to use the premises were based on an easement.

On balance, a court would probably construe S's right as either (a) a term of years for five years with rent prepaid, or (b) a tenancy at will created by S's continued possession with B's permission. In either case, the rights and liabilities of S and B will be governed by the law of <u>landlord and tenant</u>.

B. Damages

Both S and B suffered damages from the building's collapse: (a) S potentially lost the value of $3\frac{1}{2}$ years of his five-year term and his personal property, and (b) B lost the value of the entire building she bought from S just $1\frac{1}{2}$ years earlier.

1. Liability for the Structure

S as a tenant had a <u>common law duty</u> to make <u>minor repairs</u>, so as to comply with his duty not to commit <u>waste</u> whether such was the result of permissive or affirmative conduct. Normally, this duty not to commit, or allow, waste includes a duty to keep the premises <u>wind- and watertight</u>, if major structural repairs are not required to accomplish the same. Here, S failed to repair the small roof leak. He also failed to inform B about the leak. Ultimately, this lead to conditions that helped cause the building's collapse. Accordingly, B can argue that S should be held responsible for the monetary value of the destroyed building.

On the other hand, generally a tenant's common law duty to make <u>minor repairs</u> does not obligate a tenant to replace or repair a building that had been destroyed or substantially damaged by such things as fire, floods, or other acts of God. Thus, S can argue that he has no common law duty to replace the building. (It also does not appear that he has any express contractual obligation to do so, like an <u>explicit replacement clause</u> in a lease.) Under modern law, S could also argue that not only is he not responsible for the damage, but that B, his landlord, breached a legal duty he owed to S based on the <u>implied warranty of habitability</u>. Such covenants, which are implied by law into leases, require the landlord to provide its tenants with a dwelling suitable to live in.

With respect to the <u>implied warranty of habitability</u>, B can argue that it does not apply here since in most jurisdictions it is limited to <u>residential</u> property only. Here, S was using the premises for <u>commercial</u> purposes as well. Additionally, the small leaks did not make the top unit unlivable, rather they just appeared to be a minor annoyance, which S actually appeared to enjoy. S also never notified B that the leaks were a problem, or that they even existed.

On balance, it would probably be concluded that S is liable for damages based on the monetary value of the building, or the cost of replacing it, for the following reason: Where (as in this case) the type of waste (water damage) was <u>not independent</u> of S's conduct and could <u>foreseeably cause eventual destruction</u> (though probably not in the <u>exact</u> way it occurred), S could be held liable on a <u>waste</u>, or even <u>negligence</u>, theory to pay for the damage to the building to which his conduct contributed. For the reasons stated previously, the implied warranty of habitability also does not apply here, or if it does, it was not breached.

2. Liability For Rent

S might be able to get a $3\frac{1}{2}$ year rebate of the "rent" (i.e., purchase price discount), however, because his own leasehold interest was destroyed. At <u>common law</u>, a tenant was considered to have purchased an <u>estate in land</u> that continued even after total <u>destruction</u> of the <u>fixtures and improvements</u> on it, and thus the tenant was <u>required to keep paying rent</u> even after the structures had been destroyed. However, an <u>exception</u> to this general rule existed for situations where, as here, the tenant <u>leased only certain rooms in a building without</u> leasing the land underneath; in that case, the <u>subject matter</u> of the lease being destroyed, the tenant was <u>not required</u> to continue paying rent.

Further, under <u>modern law</u>, tenants are usually allowed by <u>statute</u> to <u>terminate</u> the lease upon <u>destruction</u> or <u>uninhabitability</u> of the premises. This relieves the tenants from the <u>harsh</u> common law rule, and encourages landlords (who are <u>better able</u> to do so) to obtain <u>insurance</u> against destruction.

To counter the preceding, B could argue that these types of modern statutes typically do not apply, however, where the building <u>gradually deteriorates</u> due to the elements. Here, the small leaks continued slowly for <u>over a year</u>, creating a damp condition that catalyzed a termite infestation, leading to a final sudden catastrophic collapse. Thus, if the final collapse was part of a "gradual deterioration," the statutes relieving S of a duty to pay rent may not apply. Additionally, B can argue that S was merely a tenant-at-will. Thus, he has no right to recover "rent" since he used the premises only at B's will anyway. B can also argue that if any rent rebate is owed, she is entitled to set off against this sum the money S owes her for damages to the premises caused by his conduct.

On balance, S <u>would probably be</u> entitled to a rent rebate, subject to any offset rights possessed by B.

II. B and T

A. Nature of Bonus Rent

B by written lease gave T a <u>tenancy of years</u> (i.e., an estate for a <u>fixed period of time</u>) for residential purposes. Under the written lease, T paid $10,000 in refundable "bonus rent," to be returned if the premises were in good condition at the lease's termination. B and T also agreed T could assign or sublet his interest with B's prior consent.

The "bonus rent" would probably be classified by a court as a <u>security deposit</u> designed to secure the landlord against damages she may suffer by reason of T's breach. Landlords sometimes try to make such advances <u>nonrefundable</u> by calling them "<u>rent</u>," but here the deposit is <u>expressly refundable</u> and thus would probably be held to secure the landlord from any damages T may inflict on the premises. Although the amount of this security deposit is high (usually a security deposit is equal to no more than <u>two months</u> rent), the amount involved is probably not so high as to make it <u>unconscionable as a matter of law</u>, unless the amount was expressly prohibited by a statute in the jurisdiction where the property is located.

B. Sublease/Assignment Distinction and Validity

T's "sublease" to X, if valid, is really an <u>assignment</u> since it transfers the <u>entire remaining length</u> of T's 20-year lease term to X. This is unlike a true sublease (through which the sublessor transfers less than his <u>entire remaining interest</u>, even if only by <u>one day</u>). Regardless of whether the contract between T and X is deemed a sublease or an assignment, T would remain <u>in privity of contract</u> with B and continue to be liable to B for any breach of the covenants contained in his lease with B should assignee X fail to perform, absent a <u>novation</u> or a <u>release</u> by B.

The <u>validity</u> of T's assignment to X is governed by the construction and enforceability of the contractual clause concerning assignments and subleases. In many states, clauses prohibiting transfer without landlord's consent are generally <u>enforceable</u> even if the landlord <u>unreasonably</u> withholds consent on the theory that landlord has a personal right to choose his tenant. While most leases contain a clause whereby the tenant promises <u>not</u> to assign or sublease <u>without</u> landlord's consent, T's lease provides only that the tenant may assign or sublet <u>with</u> landlord's consent but is <u>silent</u> to what happens when <u>no consent</u> is given. Since such <u>antitransfer clauses</u> are <u>strictly construed</u> against the landlord, this clause <u>may</u> be held not to prohibit transfer <u>at all</u>.

On the assumption that the clause will be construed to have some meaning and not be simply superfluous, it may be held to <u>prohibit</u> transfer <u>absent</u> consent. If so, the assignment or sublease was probably voidable by B. In some jurisdictions, however, a landlord's refusal not to allow a sublease or assignment must be reasonable. If the property is located in such a jurisdiction, the assignment or sublease would probably be valid since B's reason for not consenting (X is a scientist) was <u>totally unreasonable</u>, unless, of course, B knew that X was planning on conducting experiments in his building with termites.

In any event, B's conduct of <u>knowingly accepting rent directly</u> from X would normally be construed as a <u>waiver</u> of the antitransfer clause, thus <u>validating</u> T's assignment to X. This is probably true even though B complained each time that X had no interest, since accepting rent is <u>inconsistent</u> with such complainants.

C. Liability for Rent

T's arrangement with X provided that X would pay the required $1,000 per month rent to B for the remaining approximately 19 years of the term. Nonetheless, as explained previously, T remained liable to B for the rental and other obligations specified in his lease, irrespective of whether X paid T any or all of the monies promised to him under the "sublease." Thus, the fact that X probably stopped paying the rent to B when the premises were destroyed would not excuse T's obligation to pay B under his own lease. Further, under the <u>common law</u>, T would probably continue to be held liable for the rent since he was leasing the <u>lower unit</u> and presumably the <u>land beneath it</u>. Unless the land was destroyed, T thus still had something to possess (unlike S, who had only an upper floor unit). At modern law, the common law doctrine is generally not applied to <u>residential</u> leases, however, which is what T contracted for from B. In some jurisdictions, though, the modern rule of excusing a tenant's obligation to pay rent when the premises are destroyed is held not to be applicable to commercial lease. Consequently, because X used the premises as a research facility, even under modern law T might not be excused of his obligation to pay rent to B.

D. Liability for Destruction of the Premises

T does not appear to have directly committed waste. However, he is probably liable for any waste committed by his subtenant or assignee, X, since X was occupying the unit originally rented by T. Did X commit waste chargeable to T? <u>Waste</u> is any <u>act</u> or <u>omission</u> by the tenant that is <u>unreasonable under the circumstances</u> and <u>reduces the value</u> of the landlord's fee interest. Here, X's conduct in allowing the three termites to escape from his jar may have been <u>unreasonable under the circumstances</u>. If X was aware of the <u>unusual maritime conditions</u> (which he <u>should</u> have been because of the <u>leaks</u> and/or the <u>building's seaside location</u> in an area of <u>heavy precipitation</u>) and the <u>propensities</u> and <u>nature</u> of <u>termites</u> (which, as a <u>scientist studying them</u>, he <u>should</u> have been) he should have taken <u>unusually strict precautions</u> to <u>prevent</u> the termites' escape. To the extent X's waste led to the entire building's collapse, T is liable to B (<u>joint and severally</u> with X, see *infra*) for its value.

T may try to avoid payment of damages by arguing that X <u>did not</u> commit waste, took <u>proper precautions</u>, was <u>unaware of S's leaks</u>, and <u>could not have foreseen</u> or actually <u>caused</u> the presence of the millions of termites that caused the destruction. At the very least, T will argue, S is primarily responsible since the destruction could <u>never</u> have occurred without S's <u>waste</u>, while it very well may have without X's, since termites are rather <u>common</u> in seaside wooden structures. These arguments may have some merit depending on the extent of precautions taken by X, the <u>patent</u> or <u>latent</u> nature of the moisture problems caused by S, and the <u>presence</u> or <u>absence</u> of termites in the building prior to X's occupancy. Since the facts do not disclose the circumstances, T's <u>possible</u> defense cannot be completely evaluated. On balance, T would appear liable. If not, he would, of course, be entitled to a refund on his security deposit.

Professional Publications, Inc. • Belmont, CA

III. B and X

Since there was an <u>assignment</u> from T to X, but no <u>assumption</u> by X of the lease, and no <u>novation</u> between B and T and X substituting X in T's legal shoes, the rights of B and X are determined by <u>privity of estate</u> only.

This means B can enforce against X those lease covenants that <u>run with the land</u>, i.e., promises in the original lease or implied by law that "touch and concern the land" such as the duties to pay rent and not to commit waste. (Here, the burden of these promises affects X's <u>use</u> and <u>enjoyment</u> of the land.) The discussion regarding B's rights to rent and T's obligation to pay it apply equally to B v. X, as do the discussions of T's liability to B based on waste. These discussions will not be repeated in detail here. One additional factor should be mentioned: X should have reported the termite escape to B so that she could have arranged for proper pest control measures to be taken to protect the building and in furtherance of the implied covenant of habitation if it applies. X's failure to do so would further support B's damage claims against him for waste. B may also argue that X has no rights as a tenant because his sublease or assignment was void because B did not approve it. However, as explained previously, B probably waived any right to object to X's tenancy by accepting rent directly from him.

In response to B's damage claims for future rent and the collapse of the building, it can also be anticipated that besides arguing that he is not responsible for either because of the sudden destruction of the building from natural forces (water and insects) and B's failure to properly maintain the structure, X will undoubtedly argue that he is not liable because it is not foreseeable that the release of a few termites would cause the building to collapse, especially within such a short period of time. Moreover, X will argue, B is liable for (a) the costs of his finding an alternate comparable leasehold premises, (b) damages to his scientific equipment and other personalty, and (c) his <u>personal injury (broken arm)</u>, all incurred as a result of B's negligent failure to repair and maintain the premises in habitable conditions.

It might also serve either S's or B's interest to argue that X's tenancy was a periodic one, i.e., month-to-month. Such an interpretation of X's tenancy would relieve him of any liability for future rent. Similarly, it would relieve B of any obligation to pay for the cost of finding an alternative dwelling for the rest of T's lease term if she was found to be at fault. Specifically, either B or X could argue that, if <u>arguendo</u>, any tenancy <u>was</u> created between B and X, it was a <u>periodic tenancy</u> from month to month, created when B first accepted rent payments, since B <u>always objected</u> to the assignment of the written lease.

Should X be found to be without liability for either future rent or damages for waste, he would be entitled to a return of the bonus rent money since the lease covenant concerning such also probably <u>runs with the land</u> since it obviously affected X's enjoyment of the property (i.e., return of the $10,000 depended on returning the property in good condition, something only X could do). (In such circumstances, however, X would probably be contractually liable under his "sublease" with T to return the money to him.)

On balance, X would probably be found liable to B for any damages resulting from his unreasonable conduct in letting the termites escape; he will probably also be unable to obtain relief from his rent obligation, especially if his waste helped cause the collapse, but B would not be entitled to obtain a double recovery of future rent or damages based on the value of the destroyed premises from both X and T, and/or S.

IV. T and X

As an <u>assignor</u> as opposed to a <u>sublessor</u>, T owes <u>no duties as landlord</u> to X. X will argue the "sublease" was actually a sublease and that T actually owed such duties to X. But the preceding discussion shows that X would not prevail on this argument since T conveyed his entire remaining <u>durational</u> estate to X (assignment).

It thus appears that (a) T will seek <u>indemnity</u> from X to the extent T must pay any damages to B stemming from X's waste, and (b) T will seek recovery of the $10,000 bonus rent from X if X obtains it from B.

If T is liable to B, he will likely obtain indemnity from X since as between the two (assuming T fully disclosed all he knew regarding latent moisture conditions) the fault lies primarily with X for the building's collapse. T is liable for X's waste and other breaches of lease as a matter of <u>privity of contract</u>, but equity will allow him to seek <u>indemnity</u> (i.e., reimbursement) from X, the <u>active cause</u> of the damages.

If X recovers any of the bonus rent (see previous discussion), T will have a <u>contract</u> right against X for this sum. X may argue the "sublease" was void and unenforceable and that the assignment caused the bonus rent covenant to run with the land, making the sum payable to X. The argument appears self-defeating, since if the assignment is void, so are its terms. (X may also be <u>estopped</u> to make this argument in any event.) The correct analysis is that the assignment was mislabeled a "sublease," is enforceable and not void, and X <u>freely</u> contracted away his right to otherwise keep the $10,000 bonus rent refund as consideration for obtaining T's estate.

Answer Strategy

Marked-Up Exam

Following is an example of how a student can mark up the exam question itself so as to provide an outline for the answer and to highlight the most pertinent facts and issues.

Property Exam

S owned a three-story residential building in a seaside town; one unit was located on each floor. S lived in the upper unit, which he also used as the office for his yacht chartering business. In June 1990, S sold the building to B an elderly widow. The sales agreement provided that S could "use the upper unit as his home and office for five years without payment of rent," since the purchase price was adjusted to compensate for this arrangement."

A small roof leak developed, resulting in persistent dripping in two areas in the upper unit, particularly during rainstorms. S was very familiar with such leaks, having fixed many of them in the building during the years, but made no effort to fix this one. As a sailor accustomed to waves and spray, he felt the drips were only a minor inconvenience. He did not mention the problem to B.

In November 1990, B leased the lower unit to T for 20 years for use as a residence. The written lease required a monthly rent of $1,000 and also stated:

In addition to the monthly rent described above, Tenant shall pay the sum of $10,000 to Landlord as <u>Bonus</u>

security
deposit

anti-
transfer
clause?
ambiguous

<u>Rent</u> when Tenant takes possession of the Premises. Such
Bonus Rent shall be <u>refunded to Tenant if the Premises</u>
<u>are in good condition</u> at the termination of this Lease. . . .

Tenant <u>may assign or sublease</u> his interest <u>provided that</u>
consent of Landlord is first obtained.

what if <u>no</u>
consent?
unreasonably
withheld?
enforceable?

T paid the $10,000 and moved in.

In January 1991, X, a researcher studying termite behavior,
applied to rent the vacant middle unit. B <u>refused his application</u>
on the basis that she <u>"didn't want to rent to a scientist."</u> Later that
month, T learned he was being transferred to Iowa, approached X,
and worked out a tentative deal. T then asked for B's permission
to assign or sublease to X. <u>B refused consent.</u> T ignored this and
proceeded to enter into an agreement with X entitled "Sublease"
which provided that X would occupy the lower unit for the <u>balance</u>
of the lease term and pay the required rent to B, but that <u>T would</u>
be entitled to the refund of bonus rent. X moved into the lower
unit in February 1991. B subsequently <u>accepted rental payments</u>
from X, though <u>complaining each time that X had no rights in the</u>
unit.

unreasonable,
refused
to consent

valid?

T's contract
retains right
to bonus
rent refund—
enforceable

whole
remaining
term =
assignment
not sublease

waiver of
anti-transfer
clause

consistent w/waiver?

personal
injury
damages

X's termites?
or natives?

On December 3, 1991, the whole building collapsed a falling
beam broke X's arm. An investigation revealed that three termites
had accidentally <u>escaped from one of X's jars and multiplied dra-</u>
matically due to the unusual moisture conditions, and that millions
of termites caused the collapse of the building.

total
destruction—
remaining rent
issue

causation of collapse—X's unreasonable
conduct? S's leaks? combo? waste?

Discuss the rights and liabilities of only the following:

(a) S and B (13 points) ⅓

(b) B and T (13 points) ⅓

(c) B and X (10 points) ¼

(d) T and X (4 points) ¹⁄₁₀

Discussion of Answer

The preceding exam answer demonstrates the principle that students should underline the important parts of their answers. Professors and other exam-graders
are looking for certain "buzzwords" in an answer, such as <u>privity of estate</u>, <u>waste</u>,
<u>covenants that run with the land</u>, etc. Highlighting such buzzwords will make the
professor's job easier and will also serve to mitigate against handwriting that is difficult
to read.

The student should also note that the professor who wrote this exam specified
how much time she wanted spent on each part of the answer by assigning in the
question point totals for each subpart. Specifically, the professor's point assignment
shows that she views the answers to subparts (a) and (b) (the discussion concerning S's
and B's, and B's and T's, rights and obligations) as the most important parts of the test.
Accordingly, the student should allocate her time so that she spends roughly one-third
answering subpart (a), another one-third on subpart (b), one-fourth on subpart (c),
and one-tenth on subpart (d). As discussed previously, proper time allocation is a
crucial part of doing well on law school exams.

Professional Publications, Inc. ▪ Belmont, CA

Résumé and Cover Letter

This appendix contains a sample cover letter and résumé for a third-year law student. Their formats can be imitated by most law students in preparing their own cover letters and résumés. You may, however, want to vary the format slightly to highlight your individual strengths and minimize weak points.

Sample Cover Letter

1922 Overland Avenue
Los Angeles, CA 90025
(310) 470-6192

Ms. Sharon Y. Moore, Esq.
C.J. Communications
140 New Montgomery Street
San Francisco, CA 94105

Dear Ms. Moore:

I would like to express my interest in working as an in-house attorney for C.J. Communications' legal department. Presently, I am a third-year law student at UCLA. When I finish school, I intend to practice with a firm or company that specializes in telecommunications. Given C.J. Communications' reputation for excellence in this field, I decided to contact you for an interview.

Communication law interests me because it is a challenging and rapidly changing field. This semester I am working hard to increase my understanding of this developing area of the law. I enrolled in Professor Blackstone's Communications course and completed a Comment on universal telephone service, and I have been elected managing editor of the *Federal Communications Law Journal*. I am also considering an externship with the House Subcommittee on Telecommunications in the spring of 1993.

My work experience includes a Washington, D.C. internship with Congressman Don Jones. I have lobbied on the state level, written administrative petitions, and performed legal and factual research in the telecommunications area for several consumer groups. In short, as my enclosed résumé indicates, I enjoy working in a political environment and would feel very comfortable working for a firm that engages in a great deal of interaction with legislative and administrative bodies.

I appreciate you considering me for this position. I hope to hear from you soon. I also will gladly provide you with any additional information you might desire.

Thank you again.

Sincerely,

Joan Q. LawStudent

Encl.

Sample Résumé

Joan Q. LawStudent

Campus Address:
1922 Overland Avenue
Los Angeles, CA 90025
(310) 470-6192

Home Address:
4454 La Cosa Avenue
Fremont, CA 94536
(510) 799-8183

Education:

Law

University of California, Los Angeles
J.D. Degree, expected May 1993
Honors: F.K. Wilson Scholarship, Managing Editor, *Federal Communications Law Journal*
GPA: 86.38

Undergraduate

University of California, Berkeley
A.B. Degree, Political Science and Economics, March 1983
Graduated with High Distinction in General Scholarship
Honors: Phi Beta Kappa, Dean's List (4 years),
U.C. Berkeley Honor Society, Beta Scholarship
GPA: 3.72

Work Experience:

Miller, Starr & Regalia, Oakland, CA
Summer Associate: Conducted extensive legal research in the areas of real estate law, bankruptcy, and civil litigation. Also helped draft summary judgment motions and participated in client interviews and conferences. (Summer 1992)

Law Offices of Shari Santos, Oakland, CA
Law Clerk: Conducted both factual and legal research for firm specializing in civil litigation and entertainment law. (Part time, 1/92–5/92)

Smith and Smith, San Francisco, CA
Case Clerk: Prepared court exhibits. Indexed and organized documents. Summarized depositions. Assisted attorneys with case research and discovery. (3/82–9/82)

Don Jones' Office, Washington, DC
Congressional Aide Intern: Intern for Congressman Don Jones, 10th District, California. Responsible for analyzing congressional hearings, writing constituent correspondence, and conducting political research. (Spring 1989)

Volunteer Activities:

College Sorority President: Managed $200,000 annual budget, the group's employees, and its membership recruitment. Also negotiated a $70,000 construction contract and other smaller projects. (Chi Omega, Berkeley, CA, 1981–82)

Personal Interests:

Soccer, mountain biking, and classic literature.

About the Authors

J. Robert Arnett II currently practices law at the firm of Cades, Schutte, Fleming & Wright in Kailua-Kona, Hawaii. Mr. Arnett was admitted to the bar in the State of Hawaii in 1986 and the State of Texas in 1992. He earned his B.A. from Rice University in 1979 and his J.D. from the University of California, Los Angeles School of Law in 1986. In law school, Mr. Arnett achieved the academic distinction of Order of the Coif, graduated third in his class, and received two American Jurisprudence Awards. He also served as managing editor of the *UCLA Pacific Basin Law Journal* and published an article in that journal regarding Micronesia. In 1987, Mr. Arnett served as law clerk to the Honorable Martin Pence, Senior Judge of the U.S. District Court for the District of Hawaii.

Arthur F. Coon currently practices law at the firm of Miller, Starr & Regalia in Oakland, California. Mr. Coon was admitted to the bar in the State of California in 1986. He earned his A.B. in 1982 from the University of Southern California and his J.D. in 1986 from the University of California, Davis. In law school, Mr. Coon achieved the academic distinctions of Order of the Coif and Trial Practice Honors Board and received American Jurisprudence Awards in the conflict of laws and commercial paper courses. He also served as research editor of the *University of California Davis Law Review.* In 1987 Mr. Coon served as law clerk to the Honorable Malcolm M. Lucas of the supreme court of the State of California. Mr. Coon's most recent publication is a law review article on corporate suspension and reviver law.

Michael E. DiGeronimo currently practices law at the firm of Miller, Starr & Regalia in Oakland, California. Mr. DiGeronimo was admitted to the bar in the State of California in 1986. He earned his A.B. from the University of California, Berkeley in 1983, where he was elected as a member of Phi Beta Kappa, and he earned his J.D. from the UCLA School of Law in 1986. In law school, Mr. DiGeronimo received the American Jurisprudence Award in conflict of laws, and he served as chief articles editor of the *Federal Communications Law Journal.* He is the author of several articles in law journals and other legal publications on banking, protecting wireless communications, and mixed collateral.

Professional Publications, Inc. • Belmont, CA